Your Civil War

A Father's Guide to Winning Child Custody

By
Joseph E. Cordell

Third Edition

Your Civil War: A Father's Guide to Winning Child Custody
Published by DadsDivorce.com Publications, St. Louis, Missouri.

Front cover designed by Butch Black Designs

Photo by Getty Images

ISBN 13: 978-0-9679499-2-5

Contents

About This Book

First, let me tell you what this book is not. It is not a socio-philosophical discussion about the role dads can or should play in their kids' lives. I take it as a given that dads are as important as moms are when it comes to raising happy, well-adjusted children. Nor is this book a blueprint for political activism regarding fathers' rights, although I believe there is a tremendous need for such reforms. Finally, this book is not the key by which all dads desiring primary custody can obtain it. Winning custody is never a sure thing, but having some of the tools this book will provide you can certainly tip the scales in your favor.

Now, let me tell you what this book is about. It is a hardheaded and pragmatic instruction manual for divorced and divorcing dads seeking to maximize their role in their kids' lives. This means that as a dad, you want to ensure that you are awarded the most time and the most influence possible in the aftermath of your divorce. As a practitioner, I deal with what's possible, not what's theoretical. Therefore, I must play the hand that is dealt me by the real world. In many cases that hand is not ideal, but my challenge as a lawyer is to make the best case possible with the circumstances at hand.

This battle-hardened realism is not to be confused with resignation or acquiescence to the status quo. On the contrary, I have built my practice on a willingness to step on toes, to unapologetically challenge discrimination in the system, and to undertake bold and imaginative strategies to enhance a client's chance of success. Despite these efforts of determination and skill, however, some men simply cannot obtain primary custody of their kids. Some men may not even achieve unsupervised visitation.

You should expect the best result possible given the circumstances of your case. These circumstances include, among other things, the historical facts of your marriage, your and your wife's parenting histories, your children's ages and attitudes, your court system, and your judge. No lawyer, however talented, can create favorable facts; he can discover them, color them, and present them, but ultimately they are not of his creation. Similarly, he cannot eliminate facts unfavorable to your case. He can sometimes conceal (where ethical), minimize, shade, or explain them, but they are still there.

Regarding prejudices held by judges, lawyers, and other key players that might exist in the system, remember that your lawyer cannot change the culture; that is the chore of God and activists. However, he can take steps to minimize, neutralize, and/or utilize these factors.

Despite these impediments, however, men are succeeding in custody battles across America in even greater numbers. The lesson is that even when you do not have a balance of forces, you can still often win. You simply have to work harder than your opposite number does. Besides, what choice do you have? If your homeland is threatened by forces hostile to you and those you love, simply shrugging and walking away is not an option. The opposing forces will continue their march.

All this is to say that the objective of this book is to help you obtain the best possible result. This is the standard to which you are answerable to yourself and your children, nothing more and nothing less. You owe to your kids the most they can have of you—your time, your wisdom, and your participation in their lives. You owe them the best possible outcome.

1

A House Divided

As an avid reader of military history, I realize that litigation is, in many respects, like war. It is a war governed, as many wars once were, by rules of engagement. As I consider the type of litigation, it becomes clear that a custody dispute is a battle different from a typical lawsuit. Because these conflicts can be peculiarly bitter, passionate, and hard fought, the rules of engagement become all the more vital.

Much like in a civil war, custody battles are fought by persons between whom there had once been love and trust. Paradoxically, where such affinity exists between two people, there seems to lurk a corresponding capacity for hostility if such affection is betrayed (or is perceived to be). Add to this emotional element the very tangible matter being decided by such a war, namely the destiny of all that the combatants hold dear, and this combination makes for a highly combustible conflict.

The American Civil War occurred after an 80-year "marriage" between the North and South. The relationship over that period had been good in many respects, and the two personalities had much in common. They were also in many respects different. Over time, the sense of separateness overcame the sense of oneness, differences became more and more divisive, and synergy gave way to discord. Before the war actually commenced, various efforts were made by both sides to save the "marriage." Deals were cut, and compromises were made. Ultimately, however, the chasm of differences proved too wide to bridge, and the result was civil war.

These parallels with the principles of war will prepare you for the conflict ahead. They will serve as a blueprint for the tactical and strategic process to come. These parallels are instructive in several ways. For example, they will help you understand the psychodynamics of divorce. This helps you to both anticipate your opponent's moves and to decide on your own. These issues will be discussed further at various points throughout the book.

Some may grimace at this militaristic approach to the subject of child custody. My objective is to provide you with the best counsel I can. A military-style strategy will have you prepared and informed. A proper military analysis will ponder both the horrific costs and tremendous benefits of a fight and will counsel a negotiated peace at least as often as it dictates war. Some who read this book may choose to avoid "war" because of it. Instead, they will use its principles to obtain the best settlement possible.

I know the thought of comparing a custody battle to an actual battle is unattractive. Gaining a full knowledge of the upcoming conflict and knowing what moves to make as well as how to respond to the moves of your spouse is the best way to ensure the battle is clean, fair, and as short as possible. I agree that if a door Number 3 exists, behind which are two loving, selfless, and rational parents, that should be your choice. In the real world, however, there are often only two doors: a door behind which lurks in many cases a fundamentally unacceptable parent to whom you are asked to surrender primary custody, and a door behind which is the battle.

2

First Husbands Club

You are probably familiar with the movie *First Wives Club*. Its underlying theme was given a great deal of attention at the time. Talk shows discussed the phenomenon of men leaving the mother of their children for younger "trophy wives" Social critics lamented the condition in which such middle-aged women find themselves. The story got tremendous mileage compared with its male counterpart. The fact is that there are certain unmistakable patterns that members of both genders follow relating to divorce.

There are, of course, cases that defy stereotyping by age or gender. These are cases in which the person filing does not truly want the divorce. Given their preference, these filers would choose without pause to save their marriages. Furthermore, odd as it sounds, there are even occasions when the nonfiling spouse doesn't want the divorce either. As a result, these cases are in a sense the most tragic of divorces. I call these "divorces of necessity." They mercifully conclude marriages that simply cannot go on. Clinically, these represent a sort of marital euthanasia. In such cases, one party, and occasionally both, is subjected to circumstances or behaviors by the other that no one could long endure.

As a divorce lawyer, I will tell you that certain activities or conducts are toxic to the success of any marriage. Thousands of divorces have taught me that if such things are present in a marriage, it will never be what it should have been, whether or not a divorce occurs. I call them the "Fatal Four." These may seem obvious to you, but to give you a feel for why divorces occur and what the relative roles of husbands and wives should be, they need to be discussed. As I discuss them, you will no doubt notice that these big-ticket issues often bleed into each other. In fact, there is often a cause-and-effect relationship between them. They are as follows:

Divorced Dad's Tip:
Amid the numerous causes of disharmony leading to an irreconcilable marriage, there are four that invariably spell disaster. The "fatal four" are: substance abuse, financial misconduct, abuse, and infidelity. Any one or combination of these, in conjunction with life's ordinary complexities, draws couples like a magnet toward divorce.

I. Substance Abuse

First is substance abuse, with an emphasis on alcohol abuse. This is far and away the most common tangible thing that plays a prominent role, directly or indirectly, in many divorces. It is tough enough for two people to make it together sober, but the task is hopelessly magnified when such addictions are present. What was at best a fragile equation, a sort of delicate balance of nature, is suddenly called upon to cope with the specter, if not the fact of, legal problems (civil and criminal), financial problems, infidelities, and physical abuse. Amid all this, the user is communicating with her partner in the self-absorbed cloud that only recovering addicts or family members can vividly describe. For those of you divorcing a substance abuser, you have witnessed what I describe. You know the late hours, the selfish behavior, the violent arguments, and the infidelities to which women with such problems are particularly susceptible (or so it seems).

Although I refer here to conduct listed in the other three categories as fatal in themselves, I would hurry to distinguish the conduct of an addict as it is described here. In this case, the root toxicity is the addiction. For this category, I am referring to conduct that, but for the addiction, would not have occurred. I am not excusing the conduct. I am simply placing the fluid infidelities that accompany substance abuse and adultery in two different places in this discussion, although doubtlessly your priest or rabbi would need only one.

It is little wonder that substance abuse destroys families. Alcohol is probably the most insidious because it is legal, socially sanctioned, and affordable. Practicing divorce law prompts one to wonder whether Prohibition was such a bad idea after all.

Let me speak to you more personally for a moment. If my job in this book is to give you a bigger and better role in your children's lives, then take my advice: Get rid of all alcohol if it is an issue in your life. Do not simply cut back—quit! I was raised in a stalwart Southern Baptist home. My mother often said, referring to alcohol, that "nothing good comes of it." That advice has resonated true time after time in my practice. Alcohol is to marriage what smoking is to your body. You may smoke a lifetime without cancer. Doubtlessly you know spouses who drink and have long marriages, but for what benefit would you incur the risk? In any case, death and divorce aside, if you and your spouse drink, there is at least a substantial risk that your life or your marriage will not be what it could have been. Furthermore, and most importantly, alcohol threatens not only your marriage, but it impairs, if not poisons, your relationship with your kids. Over time, they will see a set of priorities, and a side of your personality, that will diminish your otherwise heroic place in their hearts.

TACTICAL INFORMATION

1

Get rid of alcohol if it is an issue in your life. Do not simply cut back — quit!

Some of you reading this book will find this homily a bit prudish and even offensive. I merely ask that you consider the point. Others of you will find these comments untimely, something akin to closing the barn door after the proverbial cows are out, but this issue remains important for several reasons. Some of you may still be in a position to save your marriage. Without even knowing your circumstances, I can say that remaining married would likely be better for your kids than divorce. For those of you with an alcohol or other substance issue who are destined for divorce, you are going to have to deal with accusations of abuse while this case is pending. This creates a powerful incentive for you to clean up your life. Finally, whatever happens to your marriage, you have kids to raise. They are looking to you, and this task is difficult enough while sober.

You are probably thinking that this sounds reasonable and good for problem drinkers, but that does not include you. Let me propose a simple (and what I have found to be reliable) test for whether alcohol is a problem for you. Ask yourself this question: is anyone around you suggesting to you that you have a problem? If so, you probably do.

Let me add a caveat here: if you do have a problem, do not run out and confess it or seek treatment for it without first discussing this with your lawyer. If a custody fight is looming, be sure you proceed in a way that makes strategic sense. In some cases, a public confession may hurt your case. There is no general rule here. The particular facts of your case and the court venue will dictate your approach.

II. Financial Misconduct

Irrespective of gender, age, race, or socioeconomic status, if one party persistently creates financial crises for the family, the other will eventually flee. By this, I do not mean temporary unemployment, simple bad business decisions, or some excessive spending. I am referring to chronic, financially destructive conduct. Gambling addictions and other psychiatric issues often underlie such conduct. Finances go to the very quality of a family's existence, e.g., health, safety, and housing, and no one will long endure threats to his and his kids' survival.

In recent years, this issue has arisen with increasing frequency as legalized gambling has spread. I had a case recently in which Mom took her small children with her on the gambling boats each day while her husband was at work. While she gambled, the kids were corralled in the boat's day-care facilities, a common gambling perk designed to lure parents. After she had "maxed" all the credit cards, she forged my client's name to get additional cards. As mentioned earlier, categories of causes for divorce run together. This mom was suffering from depression. Predictably, she met several men on the boats over a period of several years. My client loved his wife, but after strenuous efforts to get her treated, he had to protect himself and his kids.

I want to make clear in this discussion that when I refer to financial misconduct as one of the fatal factors, I am not referring to those all-too-common cases in which the wife is dissatisfied with her husband's income. Women, as will be discussed later, do leave men because of money (often the money of other men), but such mercenary pursuits are not to be confused with the bona fide financial crises that push a reluctant spouse to a divorce lawyer.

III. Abuse

Abuse is an overused term. In fact, it has become such a feminist watchword that no one knows what it means anymore. I am using the phrase here, however, very narrowly. I am referring to conduct so harsh and recurring that no rational person would choose to stay in such an environment. Such abuse may be physical or emotional. Because of the relatively high threshold of bad conduct as used here, there is usually an underlying psychiatric condition present. Often bipolar disorder, clinical anxiety, major depression, or some combination may be at the core. Let me repeat, if such conduct is mild or occasional, it is not sufficiently toxic to fall into this category. As with any of these areas, responsibility need not fall entirely on the shoulders of one party. The bottom line, however, is that one of the parties flees the other because of the other's genuinely intolerable conduct.

I once represented a man who seemed very low-key and soft-spoken. I will call him "Dan." Dan was an information systems manager with a large company. Before he came to me, his wife ("Pam") had filed for divorce alleging emotional abuse. No red flags went up. In our practice, Mom alleges emotional abuse in every other case. It is a cultural mantra that Mom repeats over and over during a divorce.

I asked Dan about the charge. He felt hurt by the accusation and was insistent that there was no problem. Mom had the kids, two children under 10 years of age, at that point. Because she alleged emotional abuse, not only of herself but also of the kids, the judge appointed a guardian ad litem, an attorney to represent the children. (This position will be discussed more fully in a subsequent chapter.)

Divorced Dad's Tip:
Be on alert for changes in your wife's strategy during a divorce. It is not uncommon to fight a lot with your spouse during your marriage. When she files the paperwork to start the divorce, you see a little phrase, "emotional abuse." While you were married you sought to discuss your differences loudly, perhaps even in head-to-head shouting matches. Perhaps it was not the healthiest manner to resolve problems, but many people do it. While this may have been standard operating procedure during your marriage, by both parties, once she files for divorce, you were emotionally abusive. Understand that divorce is a battle, and your wife is in it to win. Accept that misrepresentation of the facts or outright lying may be part of the equation. Be prepared to attack it head on.

I welcomed the intervention of a guardian ad litem. I knew he would investigate the matter, and I believed Mom would be quickly exposed. I felt confident in permitting my client to meet with the guardian ad litem alone. I went over with him what to expect, and he was articulate and personable. I was confident he would set the record straight and the accusations would be promptly proved false.

The meeting was set for 9:00 A.M., and my phone rang at 10:15. The client seemed reticent and told me that the session had not gone well. As it turned out, this was an understatement. Apparently, when confronted with specific allegations, my client realized they were true, and had this self-revelation with the guardian ad litem acting as his father confessor.

It turned out that my client had some deep-seated psychological problems that were far from apparent to outsiders. This condition was manifested, among other things, by intense anger. This anger was exacerbated by the exacting demands of his position. Yet in public, he was able to suppress the stresses and hostilities that simmered beneath the surface. Hence, the gracious-seeming guy who sat in my office, whose co-workers found so agreeable.

Yet at home, the picture was dramatically different. After work, he would enter the house angry. He would quickly become upset over the routine behavior of small children. Soon Dan would blow up, harshly yelling at and accusing all involved. Then he would storm to his study, close the door, and spend the evening seething there. Both his wife and his kids had become fearful and were guarded around him. His kids were confused. They often did not understand on a given occasion what had made Dad mad at them. Although they loved him, they were fearful and guarded in his presence, always tiptoeing and trying not to trigger an eruption. This was the world that emerged as Dan cried in the guardian ad litem's office.

Dan was a genuinely good man and a devoted father. He desperately wanted to save his marriage and to repair his relationship with his kids. Unfortunately, his wife had given up. The parties had tried counseling before without success. The fact is that with or without counseling, when one of these fatal four factors persists, there is a point at which the other spouse irreversibly walks away, no matter how much he or she desires to save the marriage.

IV. Infidelity

I mention infidelity last because it is the least frequent of the four, which is not to say that it is infrequent. Before discussing this issue, I want to be sure that we are clear about the cases to which I am referring. You will remember that this list, which I have dubbed the "Fatal Four" consists of those cases in which neither party can fairly be said to want the divorce. Therefore, I am not referring to cases in which, for example, your wife has found your replacement and wants out. The infidelity I refer to here concerns cases in which the faithful party wants a divorce while the unfaithful party does not. Oddly enough, the faithful spouse will rarely rush to divorce court. Upon first discovery, more practical concerns typically prevail: the children, the home, and the standard of living. Love is not extinguished so easily. Although bitterly resentful, the faithful spouse will nonetheless try to save the marriage, subject, of course, to the much-exercised right to remind one's spouse of his or her misdeeds. This is contrary to conventional wisdom, but it demonstrates a pragmatism that is probably good. What is more, this pragmatism survives a certain degree of recidivism.

This reluctance notwithstanding, infidelity deals a heavy and, to some extent, irreparable blow to the relationship. It is the ultimate betrayal, the cardinal violation of the marital "deal." If there is an area where one transgression can make a pattern, this may be it, but there are arguably different levels to this offense. It is a sort of marital felony, with varying degrees of seriousness, be it first-, second-, or third-degree adultery. If, for example, your wife is seduced on one occasion under extraordinarily exculpating circumstances, then it can at least be argued that you should forgive and move on. However, a relationship with a paramour that exists over time (be it a week or a year) is not a single incident of betrayal. Rather, it is multiple premeditated betrayals. Furthermore, these "felonies" are no longer simply sexual; the acts are now vested with romantic and emotional dimensions. It is under these circumstances that a spouse will eventually conclude that, despite his wishes, there is a fundamental character defect at work that preempts any meaningful prospect for an acceptable marriage.

This Fatal Four accounts for the vast majority of cases in which a divorce occurs that neither party really wants. In candor, such cases cannot make up more than 5 percent of divorces.

Obviously, some cases are a combination of necessity and preference, but it has been my experience that one of these two types of motives is virtually always predominant. This metaphor may better draw this distinction. One person may flee his home because it is engulfed in flames. Another may decide to sell his home because he desires another home with a better floor plan or is located in a more suitable neighborhood. This means that in the vast majority of divorces, one spouse is simply electing to do something different. Although elements of dissatisfaction clearly exist in such cases, they do not rise to the level of necessity.

Although it is true that divorces of necessity defy stereotyping by age or gender, the balance, that is, divorces of preference, do not. In fact, the great majority of divorces readily fall into one of two categories, depending on who wants out. Men and women choose divorce at different points in life and for different reasons.

Regarding men, it is not surprising to hear that if a man is going to divorce, he is most likely to do so in his forties. This is the period in most men's lives when they are enjoying more income, more success, and more respect than ever before. Furthermore, their prospects are the greatest during this period in their careers. Worsening matters further, men are often considered more attractive in their forties than at any other time in their lives. Men, it seems, are not punished for aging. I must add that this appeal cannot be that men in their forties look younger, because they fully look their age. The point seems to be that this is normal. As women view men, it must be the composite effect that accounts for their "sex appeal."

Whatever the reason, it is not surprising that men in their forties, with their egos and sex drives notoriously intact, succumb when a comparative abundance of opportunity presents itself in the form of women who are younger, more attractive, and more interesting than their wives are.

The prime-time stereotype has 45-year-old men marrying women in their mid-twenties. Although doubtlessly this occasionally happens, the norm is an eight to twelve year difference. More often then not, these men, already with teenage children, quickly start new families with their new mates. Of course, statistically the survival rate of such second efforts is even lower than that of the first. Therefore, the probability is great that such men will end up in another custody situation.

When such a man comes to my office, I can usually spot him within a few minutes of our meeting. His age is, of course, the first important clue, but this fact alone is not conclusive. He could be 40-something and yet be there of necessity, or the problem could be that he has a 30-something wife who wants a divorce. I will often ask early in the meeting, "Who really wants the divorce?" I should point out here that it is irrelevant which party actually files. Often the party who does not want the divorce is the person who technically commences the process. If my client says either "both of us" (translation: him) or "I do," then the rest is details. The bottom line is that the husband wants out. Such men compose less than 15 percent of my client base, and it is not because I turn such cases away. I believe the number is low because the myth is perpetuated by the media.

Now let us consider women: is there a pattern to be found among them in their decision to get divorced? Let us first put aside those gender-free circumstances previously discussed (abuse, alcoholism, and adultery). What is left is an unmistakable and almost invariable profile of women who choose divorce. They are in their thirties; their husbands, by the wives' own description, are decent guys; they have young kids; and, almost invariably, they have a boyfriend.

Every day I meet with a man in his thirties whose wife wants a divorce. My client is usually stunned and confused. His wife is sending mixed signals, and her reasons for wanting a divorce are vague. Occasionally, she even seems ambivalent as to whether she wants the divorce. My client desperately wants to save the marriage. His tendency is to blame himself and to irrationally focus on his deficiencies as a husband. He tends to cling to her (in effect if not in fact), repeatedly asking for another chance. He pathetically assures her he will do better. If I ask him what exactly there is for him to improve upon, he rattles off a lengthy list of his failings. As I listen, I realize these items cannot explain, even cumulatively, his wife's decision.

What my client does not yet realize, however, is that his wife's decision to surrender her family has nothing to do with him. I believe the stimulus is something much deeper. The fact is that women in their thirties are intensely conscious of aging. You do not have to have a PhD in sociology to realize that aging is of more importance and urgency to your wife than it is to you. Women in this culture (perhaps in all cultures) have not failed to notice that physical and sexual attractiveness are powerful and frequently determinate factors in their relationships with men. Therefore, there is a closing window of opportunity for women in their thirties to obtain a desirable mate. For married women this means a lateral move or, better still, the opportunity to trade up. Put differently, the cement is drying. If such a woman is not completely "fulfilled" (whatever that means), she must take steps soon to rectify the situation.

However, my experience has been that the factors discussed so far are not, in and of themselves, sufficient to stimulate a wife and mother in her thirties with an admittedly decent guy to jettison it all.

The fact is, your wife is on a boat that, despite its less than perfect accommodations, does float. As a result, it would be the pinnacle of recklessness for her to jump ship, hoping against hope not only that another seaworthy vessel will come along but also that its accommodations will constitute an improvement.

Doubtlessly, she realizes that the good guys, the desirable guys, are already married in their forties. The single guys in that age group are, for the most part, laden with baggage, such as child support, hostile ex-wives, financial problems, and alcoholism. What I am coming to is this: assuming you meet that minimum threshold of fitness already discussed, your wife will not leave you unless there is someone else. Some of you reading this book are shaking your heads. You have woven far more complicated psychological explanations for your wife's actions. This propensity is compounded by your exaggerated perception of your own culpability. I can only suggest that you wait 6 months and then reread this section.

3

Custody: Past and Present

Men commonly complain that women are treated better than men in custody matters by courts. Doubtlessly in some courts, this stereotype is accurate. It is simply a fact that we have a great deal of cultural baggage on this issue to which judges are not immune. You will probably be surprised, however, to learn that this is a relatively recent phenomenon.

TACTICAL INFORMATION

Since 1960, virtually all states have rescinded their gender-biased criteria for custody determinations.

In the early nineteenth century, children were regarded as a type of property and were awarded as such. As with other property at that time, the husband fared well. In fact, there was a "paternal presumption" that dated back to the time of the Roman Empire. The children should go, it was held, with the parent whose financial resources best equipped him or her to care for the child. Naturally, with property laws favorable to husbands, this accrued to his benefit. Therefore, a refutable presumption existed in Dad's favor. This meant that Mom essentially had the burden to show Dad to be unfit.

[1] Mary Ann Mason and Ann Quirk, "Are Mothers Losing Custody? Read My Lips: Trends in Judicial Decision-Making in Custody Disputes—1920, 1960, 1990 and 1995," *Family Law Quarterly 3* (1997).

In approximately the mid-nineteenth century, the pendulum swung in the opposite direction. Courts, purporting to focus on the welfare of the child, adopted new presumptions, the so-called "tender years" or "maternal" presumption. These preferences held that moms were better suited to care for children, particularly younger children, than were dads.

Since 1960, virtually all states have rescinded by statute their gender-based criteria for custody determinations. In fact, today virtually all state statutes expressly forbid gender discrimination in such matters. Now most state statutes proclaim the best interest of the child as their touchstone.

Despite such statutory rhetoric, however, it is simply a fact that moms have an edge in many, if not most, courts across America. This is a fact that virtually all seasoned divorce lawyers recognize, although it is difficult to prove empirically.

Divorced Dad's Tip:
Watching your wife walk away with your oak dining room table will make you grit your teeth; watching her take the house will make you pull out your hair; but watching her "take" your children will pull out your heart. A custody dispute can quickly turn an amicable divorce into a fistfight. As a man it is important to put aside your anger and concentrate on the best interest of your children. The big question is not "how can she do this to me?!" or "what will I do without my children?" The big question is "how will my children fare in this battle?" When you answer this question you will either (a) find a way, no matter how awful it may make you feel, to negotiate some compromise with your wife, or (b) understand that the anguish your children suffer in a caustic environment far outweighs your own feelings, and relent making some very painful concessions regarding custody.

The judiciary naturally is quick to deny that such arguably unconstitutional decision-making occurs. Feminists are more emphatically dismissive regarding such claims. In an often-cited article in the leading journal for family law practitioners, it is argued that the results are now balanced between men and women in custody disputes.[1] While conceding that during the first six decades of the twentieth century courts favored moms, they argue that things have changed since 1960. As proof of their thesis, they cite a study they conducted of appellate cases from four different years: 1920, 1960, 1990, and 1995. In each of these years, the authors analyzed one hundred appellate cases that were randomly chosen to see what the courts considered and what they did. Among the trends the authors cited was that after 1960, the courts rarely made reference to a maternal presumption, as was commonly the case in the cases from 1920 and 1960. The courts instead began regularly relying on the phrase "primary care giver," which is more often than not a euphemism for "maternal preference." Nonetheless, on the basis of the courts' final decisions in the above cases, the authors concluded that, "the data from 1920, 1960 and 1990 reveal remarkably little change in the distribution of custody awards between father and mother."

In the 1920s, mothers were more frequently favored as the custodial parent in appellate court decisions than fathers (46 percent to 35 percent , with the remaining 19 percent apparently representing third-party awards). According to Mason and Quirk, however, "By 1990, fathers gained on mothers and were favored equally (44 percent vs. 45 percent)... The pattern holds true for 1995 as well."

It is readily apparent that the authors are law school professors and therefore poorly equipped, based on their lack of actual experience, to best explain the cited statistics. The authors conclude that only a small percentage of custody disputes go to trial, and only a small percentage of these are appealed. Therefore, it must be recognized that the appellate sample is but an extremely small fraction of the custody disputes. Furthermore, and most importantly, the cases actually going to trial, much less those appealed, are in no sense a random sampling of divorce cases in which dads wanted custody. Pruned from the trial docket entirely is the vast majority of cases (likely in excess of 95 percent) in which a dad was discouraged by his counsel from ever attempting to obtain primary custody in the first place. Men sit in law offices all across America every day and are told (correctly in many cases) that they do not have a chance. They are told that they will spend $15,000 and likely lose. They are cautioned that the judge could get mad if they persist. As a result, they may get less and pay more.

Such men are effectively chilled from the proceeding by the process itself. Statistics, such as those cited, reflect by definition the infinitesimal percentage of cases in which the dads had particularly strong facts, particularly strong wills, and exceptionally large war chests; it is not uncommon to spend $20,000 to $30,000 waging and then appealing a custody dispute. Therefore, men that can and do go that distance are by no means representative of the typical dad with the typical budget, before the typical court.

Divorced Dad's Tip:
In most divorce cases involving custody, attorneys give their male clients some pretty practical advice: the odds of you "winning" are slim; the deck is stacked against you; the judges and supporting systems are bias against you and if your wife is just a regular ol' mother (that is, she doesn't have a substance abuse problem or doesn't beat your children), the sympathy of the Court subconsciously rests with her. As you head into a divorce you must realize that if your wife contests your custody proposal, you likely will have an uphill battle that will cost you a sizable amount. But be determined. Just because the system may favor the other party does not mean you must give in. There is no legal reason for the Court to favor the mother over the father purely on the basis of gender. If you are involved in your children's lives, why roll over and surrender?

4

The Path to War

Opening Fire: The Petition, Answer, and Cross-Petition

Although there is often a frenzy of activity before either spouse commences a divorce proceeding, the formal process begins when one of the parties files a "petition for dissolution." The petition is typically a short, simple, and legalistic document stating the basic facts (date of marriage, separation date, addresses of the parties, state residency information, and names and dates of birth of children) and a request for the relief sought, that is, divorce, child support, maintenance, and property division.

The person filing the petition is termed, appropriately enough, the "petitioner." The person receiving the petition, and from whom a response is in order, is termed the "respondent." In some states, the parties are simply called "plaintiff" and "defendant," but I suppose the majority position reflects the legislature's effort to distinguish divorce litigation from other lawsuits to perhaps make divorce litigation seem less impersonal.

The petition itself does not give the respondent much information as to what the petitioner is actually seeking. It is common to throw in a request for much more than one may actually expect or want. A sample petition is supplied in Appendix 1. When a client is served with a petition, he is often outraged to read that his wife is claiming to be incapable of supporting herself and that she wants all attorney's fees paid by her husband. She will typically ask for sole physical custody of the kids and possibly a disproportionate share of the assets. I tell clients not to panic or be offended. Although she may in fact go to war for everything requested in her petition, often it is a standardized "prayer" her attorney puts in every such petition. You might call it a Christmas wish list.

Also, states that are "fault" states may require an allegation of misconduct, for instance, adultery, physical abuse, or extreme and repeated mental cruelty, in the petition to grant the divorce. Naturally, when a good husband and father is served with a document making such allegations, he is incensed. Again, I tell him that his wife inserted the sentence solely for the purpose of getting out of the marriage; in most cases, neither she nor the court will give it any further attention. If this sounds manipulative and dishonest, it is.

TACTICAL INFORMATION 3

Don't be shocked by all that is asked for in your wife's petition. It is only a self-centric "wish list."

A process server or sheriff serves the petition to the respondent. The respondent typically has 30 days from the date of service to file an answer. The answer is usually very bland and brief. It admits or denies each assertion in the petition and will ask the court to deny the petitioner's request (see the sample answer in Appendix 2).

With the answer, the respondent often files a cross-petition. This is the respondent's counterpart to the petitioner's petition and therefore sets forth the respondent's position on the basic facts and the relief sought. Irrespective of whether the respondent actually desires a divorce, it is a good idea for him to file a cross-petition. For the respondent to mount a proper defense, he must have his own demands before the court in the form of a petition. If he did not file a petition of his own that sets out his expectations for a divorce, then he could find himself at trial, with the agenda having been set by his wife in the form of her self-centric wish list. Thereafter, the petitioner typically has 30 days to file her answer to your cross-petition.

The First Engagement

> Weigh the situation, then move.
>
> *-Sun Tzu,*
> *The Art of War,*
> *circa 2000 BC*

In any serious and important conflict, after hostilities are commenced, a series of initial skirmishes quickly follows. These test the strength and will of each combatant, and may determine relative positions for the balance of the conflict.

In a divorce, these take the form of various motions filed early in the process to place in effect orders that normally will endure for the balance of the case, that is, until trial or settlement. In many states, these are simply called "temporary orders." Other states may use arcane Latin labels, such as Missouri's "motion pendente lite." In any case, the purpose is the same: to establish some sort of stable arrangement until the case is concluded.

If you think about it, it makes complete sense that such a device should exist. As long as you were operating as a married couple outside divorce court, there were, for the most part, no rules. You did not need any. Either of you could have custody of your children whenever you wanted. You did not fight one another on the front lawn over this question. Likewise, either of you probably had an unfettered ability to incur joint debt, to transfer money, or to buy and sell assets. You had no need for orders forbidding the other from doing these things. This is the amazing innocence of marriage. This fragile, seemingly supernatural arrangement, when operating normally, works amazingly well.

The key ingredient, however, is trust. Without this, the bough breaks. The commencement of a divorce proceeding, you will not be surprised to learn, can quickly transform this orderly state of affairs into a state of anarchy. It is easier to trust one another when you look to a common future, but once the prospect of divorce is introduced, each party reverts to thinking again as an individual.

Thereafter, disputes over children, property, and other matters can, and often do, quickly escalate without some mechanism in place to maintain order until the court issues its final divorce decree. Depending largely on the jurisdiction, the time from commencement to conclusion of a divorce could be in excess of two years.

The pendente lite or temporary order typically addresses all the matters requiring attention while your case is pending. Custody and

Divorced Dad's Tip:

When you get your divorce paperwork, take a deep breath. It may have some outrageous requests: three-quarters of the property, sole custody, a million dollars a month in child support. Most likely your spouse is represented by an attorney with a "Christmas Wish List" a mile long. Her attorney's job is to ask for the sky. Through the divorce process the list is chipped away. Remember, the attorney's job isn't to do what is fair or good for you or the children. It is to get her client the most property, child support, alimony, custody and visitation as possible. Unfortunately, this is the barometer for "winning." To get items on her list, her attorney is going to make a case against you, like a prosecuting attorney makes against a criminal. The difference is your wife's attorney is not obligated to provide objective evidence. He or she will omit all the positive things you do. He or she may make exaggerated claims, outlandish accusations and blatant fabrications. If you worked long hours to provide for your family, you will be painted as an absent father, the one who never attended your daughter's dance recitals. Be prepared to respond to these allegations with an even temper. Focus on your strengths.

visitation arrangements are dealt with, as are matters of support and possession (not ownership) of the marital home. Each party is often forbidden from transferring or dissipating assets. Attorney's fees are sometimes also addressed in the temporary order. Again, virtually any matter requiring interim attention can be addressed in this order.

In addition to the provisions contained in a temporary order, statutes in virtually every state govern certain types of conduct of the parties while a divorce is pending. These statutes are automatically triggered when a petition for dissolution is filed and often forbid either party from hiding or destroying assets. Additionally, most states forbid removing the children from the custody of the parent who had custody at the time of filing or for some period before filing. This is to discourage parents from grabbing the kids on the eve of filing for divorce in an effort to be in a better position regarding custody both during the proceedings and after.

Divorced Dad's Tip:
One of the biggest pebbles in your craw will be paying your wife's attorney fees. Not only will you have to listen to absurd allegations against your character, you may be ordered to pay for the privilege. It seems even more outrageous when your wife's attorney sends you letters for every little issue. It is part of a bludgeoning process – if she knows you'll be saddled with her attorney fees, anticipate receiving letters from her attorney notifying you every time Junior has a doctor's appointment. It is a little love tap urging you to surrender. Another unfortunate truth: the system established to provide an unbiased, fair forum can be used to attack the other party.

Notwithstanding all I have said about the tremendous usefulness and importance of temporary orders in divorces, in many cases there is never a temporary order. I would estimate that one third of the divorces I have handled were completed without a temporary order.

For other attorneys, it may be closer to one-half. There are a number or reasons for neither party to seek a temporary order.

1. There may be a quick setting available for the final hearing. Most combatants can honor a cease-fire as long as it is brief.

2. The parties may each conclude that, for a number of reasons, it is in his or her interest to behave courteously and reasonably. One powerful reason is the desire to make a good impression on the court. Another may be to avoid unnecessarily inflaming the opposing party where the prospect of settlement exists.

3. Attorney's fees are always a paramount concern. A hearing on a temporary motion could easily escalate into a full-blown trial, consuming in the process thousands of dollars in attorney fees. This expense is particularly hard to justify when, as is often the case, the temporary issues are identical to those that will be heard in the final trial. People, like nations, have only so many bullets for a given war. Accordingly, they have to ration their resources.

The actual explanation is typically some combination of the above. If there is a temporary motion filed, the hearing may be very perfunctory. This is because most judges do not want more than one trial in each divorce. This is in part for the sake of the parties and in larger part for the sake of the judge. This is particularly true regarding custody and support matters. With regard to some issues, the evidence presented at a temporary hearing is the same as that presented at the final hearing.

Although judges may be forced on occasion to submit to more than one trial in a given divorce, they are determined, where possible, to not hear the same trial twice in the same divorce.

Therefore, the judge and the attorneys normally will make serious efforts to arrive at an acceptable temporary arrangement by consent of the parties. Commonly this consent temporary order will address possession of the marital home, custody and support of the kids, maintenance, protection of assets, payment on debts, and any other pressing issue requiring interim attention, but remember that your temporary order is only in effect until the divorce is concluded.

Divorced Dad's Tip:
A couple starts out planning their divorce in a logical and fair-minded manner; virtually all the details (child support, visitation, holidays, etc.) were laid out without an attorney. Once they separate, however, the wife begins receiving advice from other divorcees, many of whom apparently were victims of some really crummy husbands. These seeds enrage her over time, and all the civility flies out the window. Courts can write all the orders in the world, outlining a fair property settlement, a reasonable visitation schedule, and a workable child support amount. Surprisingly the orders matter little to your wife. The bottom line: the emotions once used by your wife in a positive manner during your marriage will now be used in a negative manner during your divorce.

Having cited above all the incentives for peaceful temporary orders, there are nonetheless cases in which certain matters must be tried. For example, if you are seeking primary or joint (50/50) custody, the temporary arrangement may be strategically critical to your success.

This tends to be particularly true when the final trial date is in the distant future. Also, if Mom and Dad are in different school districts, Dad may be disadvantaged if his children start in a new school while in Mom's care.

Therefore, a lot of analysis should be given at the outset of a divorce as to whether a temporary order should be sought and, if so, whether to compromise or fight. Of course, the other side may pursue its own temporary order and take such positions that you have no option but to have the matter tried.

Each case must be evaluated individually as to the best interim strategy. Although you do not want to unnecessarily irritate your judge (which is a factor that must be considered) or to incur unnecessary legal expenses, you must not let these concerns preempt the strategic and tactical analysis. Properly practiced, however, this analysis should incorporate all relevant factors, including your available resources and the court's likely response.

Knowledge is Power

> Foreknowledge is the reason the enlightened prince and the wise general conquer the enemy.
>
> *-Sun Tzu,*
> *The Art of War,*
> *circa 2000 BC*

After the conclusion of the Seven Days' Battle (June 25 to July 1, 1862), Robert E. Lee wrote, "Under ordinary circumstances, the Federal army should have been destroyed." That it was not was due in part to the terrain upon which the battle was fought, but even more so, in Lee's words, to "want of correct and timely information."

Information regarding your opponent is indispensable to victory. Had General Lee's reconnaissance (his information-gathering sources) been more astute, the tide of history would likely have been much different. The allocation of information can change the direction of any war. This is particularly true of a custody dispute.

Winning a custody dispute is at heart simply a matter of persuading a judge that you are a better choice for being the primary custodian than is your wife. Aside from some minimum threshold of fitness, you do not have to convince the judge that you are a good parent; you must simply appear better than your alternative. In some cases, the judge more or less holds his nose and picks the parent he finds least disgusting. This occurrence is a sad commentary on the condition of either the modern American family or the modern American judge, although I am not sure which.

This reminds me of a story. Two men were out hunting in the woods when they came upon a huge grizzly bear. One turned and began running. The other yelled to him, "What are you doing, you can't outrun this bear!" The other called back, "I don't have to outrun the bear, I just have to outrun you!"

I cannot emphasize this point enough: the objective in a custody battle is not necessarily to improve your position in the mind of the court but rather to improve your relative position. Obviously, you can improve your relative position in one of two ways: you can elevate your position or you can diminish your opponent's position. Naturally, where possible, you should proceed along both paths simultaneously.

TACTICAL INFORMATION 4

The objective in a custody battle is not necessarily to improve your position in the mind of the court but rather to improve your relative position.

Now that you understand the objective, you are probably wondering how to get there. In a nutshell, you must present to the court facts that make you look as good as possible and facts that make your wife look as bad as possible. This may seem too simple for something as convoluted as the American judicial system, and it is. In fact, judges and law school professors would be waving their fists if I failed to add some qualifications and explanation.

First, only facts meeting the somewhat complicated rules of evidence are permitted. For example, the facts must be relevant, they must meet certain criteria to ensure their accuracy (for instance, hearsay is forbidden), and they must not unfairly prejudice the court. Sometimes, facts that are only marginally relevant can nonetheless carry a bang in terms of their tendency to poison the mind of the court against your opponent. For example, if evidence in a custody proceeding reveals that Dad has a strange sexual fetish unrelated to the children or parenting, it can be very damaging.

Also, evidence may not be permitted that is unduly time consuming or duplicative. Nor will evidence be permitted that is obtained illegally or that was not properly disclosed to the other side (where such disclosure is required). Hopefully, these general rules give you a sense of the importance not only of marshaling helpful facts but also of assuring that they are of an admissible nature.

There is one more objection that this definition doubtlessly raises among the family law establishment. The fact is that it is not considered good form in such circles to speak so bluntly about the possible intention of one parent to make the other look bad in a custody battle. In addition to seeming sordid, the whole approach, critics would argue, is prone to exacerbate conflict and ill will between the parties.

Divorced Dad's Tip:

A classic tactic for Mom to gain the Court's sympathy is to get you to lose your temper. If you are only in the courtroom for one hour, and your wife or her attorney get you to erupt – it doesn't matter how – the Judge may perceive you as a villain. Many attorneys have a unique gift for provoking you on the stand, needling you to determine what gets under your skin – and then jabbing you there incessantly. Perhaps your wife waits outside the courtroom and she whispers something into your ear that galls you. She's on a mission. She's hoping you get frustrated and angry in the courtroom. That you stew in your juices before you testify. If you loose your cool in front of the judge, realize that the judge will not see the 9,999,999 hours that you are a great dad and upstanding citizen. The judge will only see you as an angry jerk that can't stay calm for one hour.

In response to this criticism, I readily concede that because the objective is to improve your relative position, it is theoretically possible to do this without attacking your spouse. However, it is impractical to implement this approach on the ground. To the extent you present any evidence at all, you are at least implicitly saying that you are better suited for primary custody than she is. As a practical matter, you should not even attempt a custody battle if you are going to make an anemic courtesy-conscious effort not to offend. Limited wars are notorious for creating the worst of all circumstances: your foe has the same level of contempt for you after ten bombing raids that he would have after 1000. All the while, she will exploit, where possible, your self-restraint. To her it represents opportunity rather than goodwill. At the end of the day, the war is lost, your foe's enmity is unmitigated, and the cost in resources invariably exceeds that of a more genuine effort.

A more legitimate discussion along these lines asks what level of restraint, if any, is dictated by strategic and tactical factors. One such factor relates to the impression that a given level of attack will make on the minds of key players, for instance, the judge and the guardian ad litem, as to both your wife and to you. In other words, what is the cost-benefit analysis?

Another legitimate basis for restraint in your attack concerns the likely ramifications for you and your child if you do not succeed. This point is different from the utopian pacifism espoused by many mental health professionals. This school of thought frowns on all custody litigation absent exceptional circumstances. Coincidentally, perhaps, such a worldview accrues overwhelmingly to the benefit of the status quo (moms).

By contrast, I am merely suggesting that if you are considering leaping across a ravine, that you first weigh the implications of ending up a few inches short. This requires consideration of a constellation of factors, not the least of which is how Mom is regarded.

Finally, I want to say a word about the common perception that hotly contested custody fights are somehow sordid and ignoble. On the contrary, most worthwhile endeavors have their distasteful moments. No one wants to crawl face down through a dung-littered pasture in Georgia or to charge, sword extended, into the black of night. All wars are replete with such unpleasantness, but the nobility and importance of the cause dwarf the many distasteful but essential tasks along the road to get there.

Now I want to focus on the means by which the parties to a divorce obtain these much-discussed facts. This process is descriptively dubbed "discovery."

The discovery process typically commences after the petitions and answers have been exchanged and may continue at various points and at various rates until the divorce is concluded.

The circumstances of each divorce dictate what types of discovery are used and when. The extent of discovery is driven by a variety of factors. Most influential, however, are the following:

The parties themselves (or simply one of them).

The complexity of the case. Is there a custody battle? Is there marital misconduct? Are bad-parenting allegations being made? Is someone alleging substance abuse?

The attorneys themselves. Some are prone to meticulous and expensive litigation, whereas others are inclined to look for ways to settle a case early in the process and, of course, at all points in between.

Discovery is the means by which you build and strengthen your case. A good case is like a brick wall: it consists of many individual bricks that together form a solid whole.

The bricks by which you improve your relative position comprise pieces of information (facts). Completing the metaphor, the mortar is the presentation of this conglomeration as a cohesive and impermeable argument.

It is worth noting that it is much more interesting to tour a great cathedral than to watch its tedious construction. Similarly, people who watch a great trial with exhilaration would be invariably bored with its painstaking and at times clerical preparation.

Divorced Dad's Tip:
During discovery, don't expect your opponent to be completely forthcoming. It is very common for one party to "forget" an account, or to claim a joint debt is really only your debt. The important thing is to remember all the assets and uncover those that your wife may be hiding.

Many of our clients have their attention focused on simply gathering information for us to present. Obviously, this is important, but equally important is anticipating your opponent's case. Remember, winning means simply beating your opponent. To do this, you have to be prepared to deal with her facts and her allegations. Your case cannot exist in a vacuum. It must consist in part of a response to your opponent's case. Discovery is a means to peek behind the curtain.

There are essentially only a few formal brick-making tools. Briefly, they are as follows:

1. Interrogatories. These are written questions sent to the other attorney for his client to answer under oath. For the most part, any question is game so long as it is relevant. The written answers must be provided within a designated time period, usually 30 days.

2. Requests to produce documents and objects. This is simply a written request submitted to the other side listing various documents of which you want them to provide copies. It can be for almost anything as long as it is relevant to the case. The other party must comply within a fixed period of time.
3. Subpoenas. These are documents sent to nonparties asking

them to provide documents or deposition testimony. Although these are often used for the date of trial, they are most commonly used to gather information well in advance of the trial date. For example, employers, psychologists, and/or school officials may be called on to give documents or testimony before trial.

4. Depositions. This is a device by which your attorney can ask questions of your wife and others under oath with a court reporter present before the day of trial. Obviously her attorney may do the same with you and others. This is typically done in one of the attorney's offices. This subject is treated in more detail in Chapter 9.

These bricks (groups of facts) can be obtained by other means as well. If you and your attorney are pursuing a particular piece of information, you must creatively decide on the best device by which to obtain it. Sometimes informal makeshift means work best, for instance, a simple telephone call and conversation with a neighbor, friend, or co-worker. Preparing for trial is about thinking imaginatively and not in terms of a few standardized tools.

In conclusion, discovery is the pursuit of information. That pursuit must be both offensive and defensive. It is about understanding both your case and that of your opponent.

5

Peace Talks: The Prospect of Settlement

To subdue the enemy without fighting is the acme of skill.

-Sun Tzu,
The Art of War,
circa 2000 BC

While your case is pending, you will likely engage in some sort of settlement discussions with the other side. Obviously, these can occur directly and informally between the parties. Usually, however, such talks are not fruitful. Alternatively and most commonly, the two attorneys negotiate their clients' positions. This may occur face-to-face, by phone, or by correspondence, which has now come to mean by fax. In some cases both the attorneys and the clients meet together in a conference room in an effort to reach an agreement. Keep in mind that such negotiations can take place at any time during the process and on as many occasions as the parties wish such negotiation. On a more formal level, however, you will probably attend at least one settlement conference (also called a pretrial conference) before trial. This is a mandatory court appearance, a sort of mandatory summit. Your and your spouse's attendance will likely be required.

The conference itself takes place in the judge's chambers. Present are the two attorneys (and the guardian ad litem when one has been appointed) and the judge. The scene likely resembles your lawyer's office, with the judge sitting behind the desk and the lawyers in the chairs in front of the desk. You and your wife will have to wait in the courtroom or in the hallway. You probably will not even see the judge on these occasions. As to the number of such conferences, this will depend upon a number of factors: the complexity of your case, the inclination of the judge and the attorneys, and, perhaps most importantly, the rules and customs of your jurisdiction.

These conferences serve a twofold purpose. They create by mandate a meeting that is calculated to afford the parties the greatest opportunity for settlement. They force the attorneys to talk to each

Divorced Dad's Tip:

If you are fortunate, your spouse will seek to dissolve the marriage fairly and quickly. If you are among the other 95 percent, prepare for a battle ranging from a tug-of-war to an all out war. At some point in the give-and-take, after some progress is made, the court may require a settlement conference. Most often the attorneys appear before the judge and present the status of the case. They will surmise what terms can be ironed out to avoid a full-blown hearing. If both parties are near a solution, these hearings are fairly brief (but not always painless). However, if there is very little common ground and key issues remain unresolved, the Judge likely will schedule a hearing. This means more time, more aggravation, and more money. This is the time for your attorney to talk turkey. If both parties are unmoving, there will be no progress. As unsavory (or even unfair) as concessions may be, the price of justice may be extremely high. Be prepared to put unresolved issues on the table and give up a little to get a little. It may go against every grain of your being. But it may be better than enduring a full-blown, bloody hearing. In life you rarely get everything you wish for.

other, with the added benefit that sitting in on the discussion is the very person who will decide the matter (the judge).

The other purpose of such a conference is, when settlement fails, to deal with issues regarding the trial: its length, the order of the evidence, and stipulations (matters relating to the trial upon which the parties can agree, such as procedural and evidentiary issues).

In other words, if there must be a trial, the court's objective (and presumably that of the attorneys as well) is to make it as quick and painless as possible. Cordell & Cordell's experience has been that where a custody dispute exists, these conferences do not usually produce a settlement. That may be because we are typically representing dads, and moms almost categorically do not surrender primary or even joint custody.

However, in the right circumstances and with the right judge, these conferences can be very effective in stimulating a settlement.

For the judge to provide meaningful guidance to the parties as to his likely leanings at trial, there typically must be at least some agreement as to what the evidence will be. At a minimum, the parties must not have fundamentally divergent views on the core facts. Clearly, it would be reckless for the judge to simply adopt as true one attorney's story over that of the other; however, he understandably can express skepticism or even incredulity regarding particular assertions. Remember that the primary purpose of soliciting the judge's thoughts in advance of trial is to give the parties a sense of what will likely result from a trial.

The above notwithstanding, occasionally the judge can give great predictive insight despite a blanket disagreement between the parties regarding the facts. Occasionally, a party's position will seem so unreasonable to the judge that he may suggest to that party that even if he were to assume as true the totality of that party's claimed facts, he would be reluctant to rule in his or her favor.

I have even had custody cases in which the judge rejected both sides' claims. In one case, my client was guilty of alienating conduct so severe that we had to concede it, at least in part. Conversely, mom had a severe alcohol problem requiring repeated hospitalizations followed by repeated relapses. The other attorney and I heatedly disagreed on most of the fundamental facts, but the judge gleaned enough from the court file and our discussion to solemnly warn us that a trial may not go well for either of our clients. We settled the case shortly thereafter.

Another sine quo non ("without which none") to settlement is some degree of flexibility in both (or at least one) parties' positions. Negotiation almost invariably requires compromise. This does not mean that you must yield on important issues relating to your child's well-being, but you might yield on unimportant issues relating to his or her well-being, particularly where an offsetting, beneficial concession is obtained in return.

Divorced Dad's Tip:

Time to reflect on the judge's opinion of you. If during the negotiation stage, the opposition makes a proposal that your attorney suggests is a pretty reasonable offer, before rejecting the offer merely on principle think of all the consequences. If the judge discovers that your rejection of reasonable offers has prevented the case from settling it may play a role in his final decision. It may also be a factor in determining if you pay your wife's attorney fees. An offer that may seem unjust to you may not appear that way to the Judge. Keep in mind their offer may be better than the judge's ruling. The bottom line: listen to your attorney. If he or she says the offer on the table is generally fair, given the way courts view things, listen to your attorney. There are instances when a settlement offer is unfair or even preposterous. If so, by all means defend your right to your children and property. But your attorney is a skilled professional who is giving you valuable advice. Time to listen!

Another essential ingredient to an effective settlement conference is a willingness by both sides to rationally assess their respective probabilities of success. This means that in those many cases in which, as discussed above, a consensus exists between the attorneys as to certain key facts, such that the judge may fairly make reliable predictions, the parties must in turn be willing to give this information its proper weight. If either side is unwilling to do this, what the judge opines is irrelevant, at least until trial.

Finally, and perhaps most importantly, as the previous material in this section makes clear, the judge is a critical component to a helpful settlement conference. His leadership style will often determine whether a case is tried or settled, which is only good up to a point. At the risk of oversimplifying, imagine a continuum of judges' management styles. At one extreme, you have a diminutive martinet that I will call "Judge A." Judge A is an intensely orderly man whose opinions on everything were calcified at birth and whose conclusions are formed irreversibly within moments of hearing a single fact. His greatest source of pride is his courtroom, where, whatever else may happen, the trains always run on time. As you might guess, Judge A runs his settlement conferences with an iron fist. You can be sure you will not walk away confused as to his position on the issues before him.

TACTICAL INFORMATION

The judge is a critical component to a helpful settlement conference. His leadership style will often determine whether a case is tried or settled.

Furthermore, an unhappy party (of which there are often two) can make things worse by insisting on a trial, which, in light of his earlier comments, Judge A would view as wasteful, unpleasant, and disruptive. Judge A's response could likely be a final order designed to send a message. Among other things, the impertinent party is often ordered to pay some portion of the other party's attorney's fees.

The above is to some extent a caricature, although I would be willing to bet that Judge A would seem disturbingly familiar to any seasoned attorney.

Regarding Judge A's authoritarian style, it does have at least a few things to commend it. There are not many trials in such a court, and in some respects, this is a good thing. The settlement conferences, although distasteful, could hardly be termed wasteful. A related point is that neither party has to anguish or speculate about what might have happened at trial.

Additionally, such judges typically run their courtrooms and their dockets (such as they are) with an iron fist, which is important to someone seeking a quick trial date. As to the judge's hardheaded and punitive tendencies, you may deem his methods eminently wise when they are in favor of your position.

If, on the other hand, the judge's position swings the other way and you find yourself having to insist on a trial, remember that irrespective of the judge's displeasure, you have a constitutional right to a trial. Furthermore, the law requires all judges to withhold judgment on every case until both sides have presented all their evidence at trial. In practice this statement of law can be, and often is, violated; nonetheless, the judge, no matter what his behavior and comments in chambers, cannot cavalierly ignore his duty without risk of reversal and a reprimand on appeal.

Silly as it may seem, it is not that uncommon for a party to reject the judge's comments and proceed to trial. Sometimes this course of action is driven by a very stubborn or hysterical client. I have been on both sides of the table with such parties. Despite his misgivings, the attorney is duty-bound to represent his client's wishes where they do not contravene his other ethical duties.

I have to add here that representing such a person in such a case is a thankless and unpleasant task. Many people cynically believe that because divorce lawyers typically get paid either way a divorce goes, they do not deeply care about the outcome. I can tell you without pause that given the gravity of what is at stake in a custody dispute and the welter of emotion that accompanies it, I would readily refuse a prospective client and his money if I knew in advance that I would be accompanying him to his execution. It is not possible to stay clinically detached in such cases. Life is too short for such unnecessary grief.

There are circumstances, however, in which a client and his counsel may reasonably proceed to trial despite a judge's unequivocally unfavorable position. An attorney may believe that the typically summary, spotty, and disjointed discussion of this case in the settlement conference fails to make his points and that after a full presentation of his case, in all its vividness and detail, the judge will see things differently. For fair-minded judges, this is not an unreasonable expectation, but you should proceed with such an expectation only where you know your evidence will be powerfully persuasive, e.g., damning documents and sympathetic, credible, and articulate witnesses. I will discuss this further in Chapter 9.

Another circumstance under which you may rationally proceed to trial despite the judge's unfavorable leanings is when you have a fairly high level of confidence that the judge will be reversed on appeal. In such circumstances the audience to which you direct your attention at trial is primarily the appellate court and secondarily the trial court. More will be said about the standards for appeal later, but for now, suffice it to say that appellate courts are slow to reverse the decision of a trial court based on the trial court's factual conclusions. A much more promising cause for appeal is faulty conclusions of law by the court.

Turning now to the opposite end of the judicial continuum, you will be greeted by a very affable and exceedingly courteous smiling face that I will call "Judge Z." Judge Z got his undergraduate degree in marketing and was the social chairman of his fraternity for three years. After ten years on the bench, he is still baffled by all this conflict around him. His biggest complaint about his job, after his salary of course, is the fact that both sides cannot always win. Nonetheless, day in and day out, he continues working to correct this problem.

Settlement conferences with this judge are part sports update, part friendly interruption, and, alas, part settlement discussion. This three-ring event typically neither commences nor concludes on schedule. In discussing the case, the judge at times alternately prods and cajoles each attorney much like a solicitous mediator, taking care all the while not to appear to take sides. At other times, the judge simply listens.

Judge Z laments his bulging docket every day. He resents the fact that judges such as Judge A do not sit through one-tenth the number of trials that he does, but then he is reassured by the knowledge that he is so well liked.

As you might guess, a settlement conference with Judge Z rarely settles cases.

He fastidiously avoids staking out clear unequivocal positions in an effort to escape giving either lawyer bad news (in addition to which he has no such positions). Therefore, both lawyers leave the settlement conference with no better sense of his probable ruling than when they came in.

There you have it: the tyrant and the unprincipled appeaser. It is unclear who is worse. Although Judge A and Z are polar caricatures, they do illustrate real-world tendencies, which among other things, will either make or break your settlement conference. Most useful would be a judge with tendencies somewhere between those of Judges A and Z. He is without bias (particularly as to gender), cautious in forming an opinion, and yet sufficiently decisive to have an opinion where he properly can. Furthermore, whatever his views, he is bold enough to express them without concern for offense to either attorney or client. In other words, Solomon would do nicely.

6

Civil War 101: Battlefield Exchanges

In addition to the previously discussed prominent landmarks along the road to divorce, there will likely be various other points of interest that should be discussed. Typically, these take the form of "motions." A motion, simply put, is merely a party's way of asking the court to give him its attention for a moment. It is like the figurative arm motion you might make to a friend to say, "I want you to come over here and look at this." Although motions can be made orally, typically they are typed documents, often less than two pages in length. Usually the relief sought is in the document's title, e.g., respondent's motion for attorney fees. However, do not confuse a motion with a petition. Petitions initiate a legal action, whereas motions are made while such actions are pending. This is technically true of motions to modify as well.

To have a motion heard, a party typically needs only to file it with the court, copy the other side, and set it for hearing. If it is nontestimonial (requiring only each attorney's argument as opposed to a hearing requiring the testimony of witnesses), the movant can probably have the matter heard within 15 days in most jurisdictions, subject to the other side's right to sufficient notice (usually 7 days). If, however, the motion is testimonial, as is, for example, a motion for

Divorced Dad's Tip:

Going to court is actually petitioning the Law (with a big L) to render a judgment. You are showing respect to a foundational institution and conceding its authority to issue judgments. Judgments should be observed. If the Court issues a judgment against you and you ignore it, you are rejecting the Court's authority. There are few things that offend a Judge more than thumbing your nose at his ruling. One of the most common contempt citations is for failure to pay court-ordered child support. The Court orders you to pay $X every month. Your response is "not in my lifetime!" Choosing to ignore the Judge's Order is contempt of Court. If the Court finds you guilty of contempt, you are in hot water. You may be fined or sent to jail. Even worse, the judge sees that you do not live up to your obligations. The judge will not be amused. If you show up in this judge's courtroom again, he or she will definitely remember you and it may affect future rulings.

contempt, the wait will likely be longer. This is due largely to the longer court time required for such hearings. Additionally, the parties typically need more time to prepare for such hearing.

A motion can be filed as to almost any concern a party may have while a case is pending. Whether it is granted is entirely another matter. Following are several motions that commonly appear in custody disputes.

Motions for Mental and Physical Examinations

In a legal action, particularly one involving the custody of minor children, either party can file a motion requesting the court to order a physical or mental examination of a party. This is often called for when a party is engaged in extremely destructive or self-destructive behavior or when there is strong evidence of a current alcohol or substance abuse issue. Some of my clients, upon hearing of such a device, are often thrilled at the prospect. Finally, what they have known for years, namely that their wives are nuts, will finally become official! However, it is not quite that easy.

The fact is that in this country, thankfully, there is a high constitutional and common law threshold that an individual must exceed to persuade a court that another party should be subjected to such very private intrusions involuntarily. In the former Soviet Union, such violations occurred routinely and without pause, but our tradition has imposed a much higher standard. I should point out, however, that the stringency for obtaining such orders seems to not only vary considerably from one jurisdiction to another but from one judge to another. In my practice, I recently had two cases in which my clients were accused of drug abuse. In both cases, there was little evidence beyond their spouses' accusations, but the other attorneys both filed motions for examinations. In one case the judge peremptorily (and correctly I believe) denied the motion, and in the other the judge granted it, simply shrugging his

---

Divorced Dad's Tip:

In recent decades the veil of spousal abuse has lifted to reveal a lot of people (men and women) abuse their spouses. While there is a genuine need for orders of protection, there are abuses of this legal protection. Realizing the courts often assume that allegations of abuse are valid, some unscrupulous women have feigned fear in order to obtain orders of protection with the hope it will give them a tactical advantage during divorce. In many jurisdictions a woman doesn't even have to be threatened. She need only claim to be afraid of her husband. Avoid being alone with your wife, if you believe she may cry "abuse." There are plenty of cases where women set their husbands up. As hard as it may be to believe that your wife of ten years could do such a thing, do not assume it cannot happen.

---

shoulders and saying that where kids are involved, it is best to be safe. The latter is the exception, not the rule. Strong evidence is usually needed for this motion to succeed, although the level of stringency may vary from one jurisdiction to another.

Motions to Compel Evidence

Another motion commonly filed is one to compel discovery. You will recall, from the earlier discussion, the critical role that discovery plays in preparing a case. Naturally, when a party refuses to answer interrogatories or to produce documents properly requested within the time required, the requesting party must have a means to force compliance: this is it.

In some of these cases, the opposing party will have filed an

Divorced Dad's Tip:

Orders of protection have, over time, seen a growing abuse by women who simply want to gain an advantage in a custody case. There are genuine cases of men threatening or abusing women, but unscrupulous women (who have no fear whatsoever of their spouses) have cried wolf to obtain an order of protection. Their sole purpose for doing so is to prejudice the Judge against the father during a custody battle. It is a mean spirited, deceitful practice by, well, there's no kind way to say it, pretty despicable people. A woman can make a false allegation and the Court in good faith jumps to her defense and becomes a pawn in her game. The man may be removed from his home and children. The Judge in the case now has "evidence" that he is not an upstanding citizen. If you have any suspicion that your spouse is being underhanded (i.e. planting evidence, reneging on agreements, fabricating statements), you should consider whether or not she is a person who believes that the end justifies the means. If she "would do anything" to "get" her children, you should exercise caution in dealing with her.

objection to the discovery sought, e.g., questions or documents, whereby he asserts a legal basis for his refusal. As already discussed, there are various limitations on the information either side must provide. Requested information may be privileged, which means it is protected from disclosure, or it may be unduly burdensome or intended simply to harass. I should emphasize here, however, that the rules of discovery are deliberately very broad in contrast to the rules of evidence, which seem to many as being unduly restrictive.

If, after hearing both sides, the judge finds in the moving party's favor, the court has the power, among other things, to strike (throw out) the wrongdoer's pleadings (a very harsh step) and/or to award the moving party his attorney's fees for the hassle. In the real world, if it is a first offense and the opposing attorney offers some minimally plausible excuse, the court will simply give his client a new deadline with which to comply without sanctions. When my client is the moving party, he is understandably angered when this happens. From his perspective, he is out additional attorney's fees while "she does what she pleases without penalty." What can I say? However, when the shoe is on the other foot and my client has not complied, the practice seems eminently fair.

Motions for Contempt

This motion may be best explained by analogy. As we go about our lives each day, we are required to do so without violating any of a host of provisions called statutes. If you do violate one of these provisions (depending on its nature), you will be charged with a crime. You will be tried and, if found guilty, punished.

Contempt, like a crime, involves the violation of a provision, but unlike crime, the violated provision is contained in a judge's order rather than a statute. In both cases, however, the repercussions can be mild to severe, from a simple warning to incarceration.

As the above implies, however, for contempt to exist, the court must have issued an order. This could have occurred at various points on various subjects. While a divorce is pending, the judge may issue an order to attend parenting classes, to pay fees to a guardian ad litem, to pay support, to permit visitation, to stay out of the marital home, or to hand over documents or other items among other things.

To be found in contempt, however, it is not enough to simply prove that the order was intentionally violated. It must also be shown that the accused party had the ability to comply. This second step is essential to fair play. For example, if a man is brought before the court on a motion for contempt for nonpayment of support but can demonstrate that he is unemployed through no fault of his own, he will not and should not be found in contempt.

Divorced Dad's Tip:

Here's a good example of biting the bullet. If your spouse requests an order of protection against you (alleging you threatened her), in the long run, you may be better off not contesting the request. Most men who have done nothing wrong will never willingly accept this. They will fight these ridiculous allegations. However, with the law it often has less to do with right and wrong than with "what happens if...." What if you contest the request and the Judge proves to be one who usually wishes to "err on the side of safety"? If there is a possibility the Order of Protection will include provisions which restrict or eliminate visitation, then agreeing to an Order that does not restrict your visitation may not be a bad idea. You also want to consider what evidence your wife will produce in order to obtain the protective order. If you believe it may be damaging to your custody case, then it may be worth agreeing to a protective order in order to keep the evidence out. This is especially true if the Judge hearing the protective order will hear also the custody case. After careful consideration and discussion with your attorney, decide whether it is better to accept (without admitting wrongdoing) an order of protection.

An action for contempt may be based on your final divorce decree (order), as well as the interim orders discussed above. Irrespective of the county or parish in which your matter may be heard, your judge will take great offense to violations of his orders. I caution clients that, despite the temptation and often the provocation, they must not jeopardize their case by flouting the judge's orders.

The consequences for contempt are largely up to the judge. However, contempt as used in this context is "civil," as opposed to the criminal analogy used above. There are several important differences. Obviously, one creates a criminal record and the other does not. Most importantly for your purposes, however, is that unlike criminal penalties, the court in a case of civil contempt can only issue orders that are reasonably calculated to stimulate compliance by the "contemnor." In other words, they cannot be simply punitive, as in criminal cases.

This criteria nonetheless often permit incarceration and other harsh remedies. Contempt is discussed further in Chapter 12.

Orders of Protection

Another motion commonly filed in or in conjunction with a divorce proceeding is that for an order of protection. In some cases, its provisions are incorporated in the temporary order and made part of the dissolution action itself. More commonly, however, the "victim" will file a separate action, in which case it is denominated as a Petition for an Order of Protection.

The order of protection is one of the most useful tools currently available to moms in divorce. As a result, it deserves detailed discussion.

Like many good intentions gone awry, the order of protection seemed reasonable enough when first adopted. Although its language is gender neutral, its purpose was clearly not. However, even that would be okay if it only affected men who in fact were physically abusing their wives or girlfriends.

As it exists today across America, the order of protection is a quick, cheap, and powerful weapon used routinely by women in divorces for reasons completely unrelated to an actual fear of abuse. It has become the gender-specific trump card of which all wives and husbands are aware. It is the ultimate "gotcha."

An order of protection is a device that women typically obtain without an attorney. In fact, at taxpayer's expense there are very helpful people at the courthouse whose job it is to assist women in completing the simple form. If the correct words are used (a vague but popular incantation is "I fear for my safety"), a judge will sign an order that day giving the wife exclusive possession of the marital home, its contents, and such other items as she may enumerate. In addition, the wife is typically awarded exclusive custody of the children.

To give you a sense for the breadth of the term "abuse," here is the definition Missouri uses in its adult abuse statute.

> **455.010. As used in sections 455.010 to 455.085, unless the context clearly indicates otherwise, the following terms shall mean:**
>
> **(1) "Abuse" includes but is not limited to the occurrence of any of the following acts, attempts, or threats against a person who may be protected under sections 455.010 to 455.085:**
>
> **(a) "Assault", purposely or knowingly placing or attempting to place another in fear of physical harm;**
>
> **(b) "Battery", purposely or knowingly causing physical harm to another with or without a deadly weapon;**
>
> **(c) "Coercion", compelling another by force or threat of force to engage in conduct from which the latter has a**

right to abstain or to abstain from conduct in which the person has a right to engage;

(d) "Harassment", engaging in a purposeful or knowing course of conduct involving more than one incident that alarms or causes distress to another adult and serves no legitimate purpose. The course of conduct must be such as would cause a reasonable adult to suffer substantial emotional distress and must actually cause substantial emotional distress to the petitioner. Such conduct might include, but is not limited to:

a. Following another about in a public place or places;

b. Peering in the window or lingering outside the residence of another; but does not include constitutionally protected activity;

(e) "Sexual assault", causing or attempting to cause another to engage involuntarily in any sexual act by force, threat of force, or duress;

(f) "Unlawful imprisonment", holding, confining, detaining or abducting another person against that person's will.

At this point, you are probably wondering what is in place to prevent you from doing this to her first. First, it is fraudulent and dishonest. The fact that your wife may be willing to do this does not justify your doing it. Second, and I suspect more persuasively, the statute, despite its claims and appearance of gender-neutrality, was created for women, and everyone in the system knows this. Therefore, when a man strolls in requesting an order, he will likely be scrutinized by the court in a way in which his wife would not. Do not misunderstand me; I am not saying that men cannot get orders of protection. They can and they do. I am merely pointing out that, at best, men can only get them when they genuinely should have them.

Once a wife decides she wants an order of protection, she normally applies for and obtains it in less than an hour, seven days a week. Furthermore, the husband, although he may be readily available and eager to respond immediately to the allegations, is entitled to no notice. He first becomes aware of his predicament when a police officer comes to his door or greets him when he returns home from work. The officer will often give him a few minutes to gather his toothbrush, a razor, and a few other personal effects. If the kids are there, they will typically wonder what's happening. At that point, the officer escorts Dad out of the house and waits until he pulls out of the driveway before leaving.

This scene is played out every day in every county across the country. For some counties, there are numerous such scenes per day.

One has to wonder what portion of these thousands of cases represent what could reasonably be termed "abuse" or the genuine threat of abuse. To my knowledge, however, no such statistics exist. Based on our firm's experience, which includes perhaps thousands of such cases, I would estimate that no more than 5 percent of such actions are even arguably legitimate.

Women's groups and segments of the legal system minimize the peremptory treatment given Dad on the front end by pointing out that the statute affords him a speedy hearing.

It is true that the ex parte ("without the other party") order that the wife obtained at the outset will only stay in effect until the "full order" hearing (or in some states, the "plenary" or permanent hearing). That should occur within 15 days thereafter, although the number of days may vary from one jurisdiction to another. This is the hearing at which Dad is purportedly given his constitutional right to be heard, his proverbial day in court. Then, after hearing both sides, the court will either deny the petition or issue a full order, which, depending on the jurisdiction, will remain in effect for a period of two years.

Assuming for a moment that a hearing does in fact take place within 15 days, which, in my experience, it often does not, such a provision nonetheless fails to adequately consider the likely emotional devastation the respondent experiences in being summarily ejected from his home and kept from his children. Furthermore, the statute permits the ex parte period to be, and often it is, extended by the court for "good cause shown."

Regarding the eventual hearing, the order of protection docket on any given day might consist of twenty or more cases, for which the judge has likely allocated less than 15 minutes each. As each case is called, the parties typically file forward and stand before the bench as each states his or her case, and that is it, the much-touted constitutional moment on which these men had pinned their hopes.

The judge issues his order on the spot. In an overwhelming majority of cases, the full order is granted. This is true for several reasons. First, and I believe primarily, it is simply a self-preservation instinct felt by many judges. On this subject, however, although I strongly disapprove of such reasoning, it is certainly understandable given the downside risk of a bad decision. As one judge once characterized his predicament in such hearings, "For me, in every hearing, it's guess right or die." He is referring to the fact that if he errs on the side of denying an order and the petitioner subsequently suffers the fate of Nicole Simpson, the fallout for him would be immeasurable, personally, professionally, and financially. On the other hand, if he errs on the side of granting the order, the downside is that Dad cannot move back into his house, and he will have to see his kids in accordance with a temporary custody schedule. However, if things are this bad between them, the judge probably figures, such orders are on the horizon anyway. I have heard it put this way, "If these people are getting along so badly that they are in this court, it's probably best for everybody if they stay apart." Unfortunately, this is a widely held rationale. I want to interject here, in all fairness, an expression of gratitude to those many judges (although perhaps not a majority) who do the right thing without regard to politics or personal fallout. As for the others, we must keep pressing our cases.

"Wait a minute," you are probably thinking, "what about this idea that we are a nation of laws and all that constitutional stuff I learned in my high school civics class? Where does that come into play?"

The celestial place to which you at least theoretically turn when disappointed by mere men in the trial court is the Court of Appeals, but there is a purely legal problem to that approach, as well as a purely practical one. The legal problem is that the appellate court defers greatly to the trial court on questions of fact, allowing the trial court to give the weight it thinks appropriate to the evidence. In this case, the evidence resides on a ten minute tape. If, during that ten minutes, the wife tosses out a claim that, if believed, would meet the extremely broad statutory requirements, the appellate court would be obliged to affirm the ruling unless some other defect exists, which leads to the next point.

The purely practical problem relates to the feasibility of appealing such an order. Even if there is a reversible defect in the order of protection, if you launch an appeal, it could easily require a year or two to complete. Furthermore, although you consider it highly improper, the judge's statistical assumption about the course of your relationship is probably accurate. Before your appellate process is completed, there is a good chance the order of protection will have expired, you will be divorced, and some new order will be in place regarding your house and your kids. Incidentally, the orders of the divorce court trump those of the order of protection court, assuming, of course, that there are two courts involved. Finally, there is the cost of an appeal. It is not unusual to spend $5,000 to $10,000 for an appeal. You must also consider the probability that you will be paying a divorce lawyer thousands of dollars during the same period that you are having to pay the same or another lawyer for your appeal. I have found that when divorce litigation commences, the annoying grease fire in the back yard grill quickly surrenders your attention to the inferno threatening your home and possessions.

As is hopefully apparent from the above discussion, it is best, where possible, to avoid an order of protection fight entirely. I realize that for some of you the fight is unavoidable, either because it has (or will) appear completely without warning or provocation or because you were conscious of the risk but for reasons relating to your custody goals made a calculated decision to stay.

However, many men who are served with orders of protection do not fall into either of these categories. In other words, they are living in a situation with a person who they recognize is highly volatile. There have often been previous ugly confrontations that are discernibly escalating. In many cases, the wife has, even on previous occasions, voiced her intention to get an order of protection. Men in this situation should promptly consult with their attorneys. They must carefully weigh the strategic advantages of staying in the home against its potential downside (of which more will be said below), and then they must contrast this with the implications, good and bad, of a preemptive move. As suggested above, custody concerns will, in some cases, warrant the risk accompanying a decision to stay. The factors governing custody are discussed in a later chapter. I must add here that grounding the decision simply on principle, although seemingly noble, is certainly not wise.

TACTICAL INFORMATION 6

Men must carefully weigh the strategic advantages of staying in the home against the downside of potential conflicts.

If, for whatever reason, you do decide to stay, you must not—and I cannot emphasize this enough—allow yourself to be drawn into any conflicts with your wife. It is bad enough that she may file an order of protection with no basis whatsoever, but do not worsen the case by giving her raw material amenable to misrepresentation. I would also recommend to those electing to stay in a high-risk home, that they document, to the extent possible, any improper conduct or statements by their spouse. A discreetly kept journal is usually helpful. If threats are being made, where legally permissible, you might record them. Finally, if your wife engages in conduct constituting abuse, you should be prepared to enlist the order of protection statute in your favor. Discuss this first with your attorney because it may or may not be advantageous to you.

Turning to those for whom preventive measures are no longer of use, at the risk of oversimplifying, you essentially have two alternatives open to you.

The first and most obvious is to fight. You know, however, that the order of protection forum does not naturally lend itself to serious and fair litigation. This is not to say, however, that you must lose. To have a realistic chance of prevailing as a male respondent in a full order or protection hearing, you need at least one of the following factors in your favor.

1. You need a judge that will at least entertain the idea of ruling in favor of a male respondent. In other words, he must have at least a threshold of evidence that Mom must satisfy to get her full order. The adult abuse statute in Missouri, which is typical, requires the judge to determine that there is "good cause" before issuing an order of protection. This phrase is defined as "an immediate and present danger of abuse." However, "abuse includes but is not limited to the occurrence of any of the following acts, attempts or threats against a persona who may be protected under [this act]." Listed thereafter are assault, battery, coercion, harassment, sexual assault, and unlawful imprisonment, with definitions for each.

2. You need a badly prepared petition for the full order. The petition is the paper on which Mom lists her complaints. If Mom fails, either by ignorance or inattention, to plead facts that meet the statutory requirements mentioned above, or if, at the full order hearing, she fails to allege anything that meets the requirements mentioned above, the petition should be denied. Sometimes she will try to compensate for a badly prepared petition by inventing new allegations at the hearing. With a proper objection, she may be limited in her testimony at the hearing to her original complaints. This is only fair. For you to adequately prepare for trial, you need to know the charges in advance of trial. Judges go both ways on this issue.

3. You should have an attractive appearance and be able to testify well. By this, I mean you should look and speak well, and have no incriminating history, particularly one that might relate, even indirectly, to violence. A smaller physical structure also helps.

4. The wife should possess characteristics antithetical to those listed above, e.g., disrespectful. Being somewhat obtuse does not hurt either.

5. Finally, you should have the facts on your side. I want my client to be squeaky clean of the charge, assuming it constitutes abuse. I wince when I hear "but I didn't push her that hard," "she hit me first," "I don't remember doing that," or, worst of all, "but it wasn't even loaded." These statements are not helpful.

In other words, generally speaking, I would prefer to deal with complete fabrications by the wife than with half-truths that force my client to make grudging concessions.

You should be warned that a decision to try an order of protection is in most courts very different from such a decision regarding other matters. A trial, depending on the issues, requires some amount of time, be it one hour or one week. A trial typically proceeds in accordance with the rules of procedure and the rules of evidence. A trial typically includes witnesses in addition to the parties and exhibits.

Contrast this with the above description of an order of protection hearing. If you have an insistent but courteous lawyer, the court may grudgingly yield to you some additional time, although not much. Lax rules tend to be an established practice in many courts. As to presenting witnesses and exhibits, you may be pushing too far. Keep in mind that the judge is probably not pleased with the bottleneck that you have caused in his already over-populated docket. It is immediately apparent to him that you intend to present a case that will significantly exceed its allocated ten minutes.

Keep in mind that the matters in dispute extend beyond the propriety of the order of protection itself. Typically, the wife includes demands relating to various other matters, such as custody, child support, maintenance, and possession of vehicles, in her petition. The judge's policies regarding these supraprotection issues vary from court to court and state to state. However, it is safe to say they are unanimous in their determination to avoid getting bogged down in a quasi-divorce proceeding.

To their credit, most judges quickly realized that wives were using orders of protection as shortcuts to, in many cases, things they would otherwise get only after a long and expensive divorce process. Courts responded to this problem, however, in different ways. Some refuse to entertain any issues beyond the bare order itself, i.e., the protection provisions, absent exigent circumstances. Others have the policy that if a divorce is pending at the time of the full order hearing, they will only consider the bare order itself. This position seems eminently reasonable, given the fact that all the other matters are already before another court or, in some cases, the same court but the wrong docket.

Other judges will address certain issues but not others; for example, if a divorce is not pending, many will feel obliged to address child-related matters, such as custody and support. Naturally, you will insist on some provision ensuring access to your kids.

This concern simply magnifies the earlier point that order of protection hearings typically do not afford the respondent an adequate opportunity to be heard. The hearing previously denied the respondent as to the ex parte hearing compounds the problem.

The decision as to whether to insist on a trial at your order of protection hearing must be based largely on what you anticipate will be your judge's policy regarding the various issues discussed herein. You should also consider his likely position on the nature and extent of your hearing and the issues he will entertain. Usually, each judge's policies on orders of protection are widely known among the divorce lawyers in the area.

What if, you may be wondering, you discover that your judge is notorious for simply calling the parties forward, asking them a few questions, and then granting the full order, ignoring, we will assume, any ancillary matters?

One possibility, assuming your time has not elapsed, is that you could file a motion for a change of judge. In most jurisdictions, you get one change as a matter of right. Be careful, however, that you do not go from bad to worse. Also realize that your motion may delay your full order hearing. One other consideration here is whether your jurisdiction's policy is to keep orders of protection and divorces with the same judge. If so, you may have a bad order of protection judge who is known to be friendly to dads in divorces. If you will recall the possible reasons that judges often grant orders of protection, this combination does not seem so contradictory.

It might be that you conclude, for whatever reason, that it is not in your interest to have a trial on the order of protection. In the interest of candor, I have to add here that, in addition to all the systemic reasons discussed above, your reason may be that you did in fact abuse her.

You technically have only one alternative to trying that matter, and that is to enter into a "consent" order.

What possible incentive, you are probably wondering, could there be to do this: why not at least put up a fight? Most of my clients initially react this way when I speak of "consent," but hear me out.

One incentive might be an offer from the other side of more favorable terms in the order than you would likely get at trial. Remember, the order of protection often covers a variety of topics in addition to the protection matters; the court may address child support, child custody, maintenance, attorney's fees, and possession of vehicles, for example. To avoid a fight, your wife may make favorable concessions in these areas.

Additionally, for some clients, attorney's fees are a critical issue. They expect to spend thousands in the divorce and accompanying custody battle and must ration their resources. Depending on the court and the circumstances, a serious battle could eat up several thousand dollars.

There is yet another more important reason for seriously considering a consent order. There was a time, not more than ten years ago, when divorce lawyers and their clients could regard orders of protection as annoying sideshows in a divorce proceeding. In the early 1990s, however, the phrase "domestic violence" weaved its way into the public policy lexicon. States began revising their civil and criminal statutes to deal with this putatively epidemic phenomenon. In particular, most states revised their statutes relating to custody so as to require a court to consider domestic violence as a factor in awarding custody. Furthermore, orders of protection were expanded in scope and duration.

States developed a scheme of reciprocity by which an order issued in one state is enforceable in another. Violations of orders of protection became criminal offenses and, in certain cases, felonies. Predictably, the federal government chimed in, passing the Violence Against Women Act of 1994.

Additionally, a finding of domestic violence has professional ramifications. It can affect one's eligibility for certain state and federal jobs, as well as a growing number of positions in the private sector.

Avoiding a determination by the court of guilt of abuse can prevent many of these adverse effects. You do this by declaring to the court at the outset of your hearing that you do not object to the order of protection being issued.

In doing this, you are not making any admission of wrongdoing. In many states, this will be indicated on the order itself.

Regarding the other issues your wife raised in her petition (child support and custody), these can be preempted in most courts by filing a petition for dissolution before the hearing date.

The result of this approach could be that you are left without access to your children for a period, although your wife's lawyer would likely caution her that flagrant mean-spiritedness sends an unflattering message to the court.

In any case, however, you would be able to obtain relief by way of a pendente lite hearing in your pending divorce. Furthermore, the pendente lite provides a much more favorable setting for dealing with such issues than does the cattle call previously described, not to mention the simple fact that a man standing before a judge in an abuse case is not ideally positioned to assert his custody concerns.

There seems to be some impulse in at least many of us that insists on some degree of just treatment. Consequently, when that fundamental standard is not met, our initial reaction is to come out swinging. Heap onto this the factor of "lover's betrayal" and the presence of children, and that reaction grows exponentially.

This describes the initial attitude of most of the men I have represented in order of protection hearings, excluding, of course the small percentage that were in fact guilty of the abuse alleged. However, these attitudes typically changed as I emphasized to them that wars are won by those who keep cool heads in battle and that means every battle. Your order of protection hearing is simply one of the battles in your civil war. If handled properly it can usually be either won or neutralized. In any case, you want to ensure that the order of protection does not become an important victory for your opponent.

Bring your lawyer into the loop the day you are served. Then, after carefully considering all the factors discussed above regarding the trial option, including not only the probability of winning but also the ramifications of losing, you should weigh these against the consent option. Then you must make your decision and not look back.

The Trial

> The Trial War is the remedy
> our enemy has chosen.
> Let us give them a full measure of it.
>
> *-General W. T. Sherman*

Unless you reach a settlement somewhere along the way, the final crowning event, the culmination of all that has come before in the litigation process, is your trial. Experts tell me that fewer than 5 percent of all divorces go to trial. This statistic, although perhaps technically correct, needs further refinement to be useful to you as a predictive tool. It may be helpful to add that on the basis of my firm's experience, if only the divorces of middle-and upper-class clients with children were considered, the percentage would at least double. If the sample were limited further to include only cases in which mom is a homemaker, and the marriage has lasted in excess of ten years, the percentage going to trial would probably double again. These percentages simply serve to illustrate that there are certain issues that are notoriously litigious in divorces, even in those in which both parties are trying to be reasonable. Although it is a basic truth that money is the root of much conflict, no issue is more fertile for litigation than that regarding the custody of children.

Additionally, a dispute over child custody is more likely to be tried than other issues, partially because the criteria for awarding custody are not sufficiently concrete and objective to permit reliable forecasting. Additionally, prognostications aside, the parties may have a genuine disagreement about what is in the child's best interest. It should be noted that by definition a custody battle means that a dad is competing with a mom for additional participation in a child's life. Women, with few exceptions, fight these battles without regard for the

Divorced Dad's Tip:

You may assume that most heated divorces center around the topic of money. The truth is that the most hotly contested issue in divorce is child custody. Often (and sometimes to the detriment of the children) the children are unwitting participants in one or both parents' scheme – not to lose "possession" of the children or, worse, to deprive the other parent of the children. A particularly sad commentary, some people seek custody primarily to use the children as a revenue stream, not because they value their children and want to nurture and educate them. Divorcing dads should develop a very clear focus. Your primary objective in divorce should be to create the healthiest environment possible for your children. Often that means having as much contact with both parents as possible. If you are a good father and love your children, do not roll over and simply allow someone to remove them from your life. Be aware that divorce can be a negative experience for your children, so try your best to insulate them.

probability of success. Let me digress here a moment to make an interesting observation. My theory regarding this phenomenon, which I must concede is entirely impressionistic, is that in addition to the love of a parent for a child, women feel a tremendous societal expectation on this issue that men do not. Women, I believe, tend to worry that they will be stigmatized in the minds of family and friends for having lost custody of their kids.

Men, by contrast, operate under a damaging cultural stereotype. As a result, I think it can reasonably be argued that if a dad is seriously (which means expensively and unpleasantly among other things) pursuing custody, there might be less reason to question his motives than those of mom.

If your divorce does make its way to trial, the court will likely have set aside in advance a given period of time for you and your spouse to present your case. The rules on this point vary widely from jurisdiction to jurisdiction. Furthermore, individual judges often have their own such policies. Judges often impose very inflexible and restrictive time constraints on their family law matters and in some cases assign to each side a specific time allotment within which each must present all of his or her evidence. Such judges fastidiously monitor each side's time, which is deemed to run whenever a given side is presenting its evidence or conducting its cross-examination of the other side's witnesses. The time allotted under such a regimen will vary from case to case. I should add that the attorneys in each case are virtually always permitted some role in this determination, although some judges often overrule time requests they deem excessive. There are certain due-process guarantees afforded litigants by state and federal law that limit the extent to which judges can deny you time for trial. Unfortunately, that limit is unclear. By contrast, some jurisdictions and some judges within jurisdictions place virtually no time constraints on a given trial. I have found that rural judges are more likely to operate this way than their urban counterparts are. This approach has its problems. Some attorneys seem to drone on eternally if permitted. Because your court is likely to impose some form or degree of time constraint on your trial, it is important to ration your evidence accordingly. Remember, your trial will likely cover more than simply child custody and support issues.

Part of the time is likely to be consumed by evidence relating to such matters as maintenance and property division. In fact, these financial issues can easily monopolize your trial time if you let them. The evidence relating to these topics normally includes various financial documents. It is not uncommon to have twenty or more such "exhibits," coupled with typically detailed testimony regarding each party's statements of income and expenses and assets, and liabilities (see examples in Appendix 3). Also, the testimony of experts, such as certified professional accountants, appraisers, and occupational therapists, may be needed as well.

Therefore, depending on the number and complexity of the issues, your trial may last anywhere from a few hours to a few days (and in some cases, a few weeks). As mentioned earlier, the attorneys may be able to settle some of the issues in advance of the trial. This can free up precious trial time. I have found such partial settlements to be helpful in another important respect. If my client's overwhelming priority is custody, as it often is, prior settlement of other issues allows me to better focus my attention both before and during trial on what is important. More importantly, however, it ensures that the judge will do the same. I think this added focus is usually more beneficial to men in custody disputes than to women. Perhaps this is because Dad often has to address reservations. Now we should focus on how you must use the time given you, however long or short it may be.

As previously discussed, a trial is your opportunity to present your best evidence (facts and expert opinions) to the trier of fact (in this case, the judge) in the most persuasive way possible (with the most powerful arguments you can muster).

As you might guess, this would rarely mean that your attorney would present to the court all your favorable evidence. Remember, you are likely operating under some sort of time constraint. Additionally, you want to present a vivid and comprehensible picture. Too many facts simply distract and confuse. At best, you lose the court's attention, and at worst, the judge effectively punishes you in his decision. This issue often comes up in custody litigation, during which clients often have the expectation that every person who may have anything remotely helpful to say will be called to testify at trial. Theoretically, this may seem reasonable, but in practice it is disastrous. In addition to the fact that both the court's attention span and your trial time are finite, if you are like most clients, your funds are finite. Without thoughtful discretion, you can easily triple your litigation costs, all the while effectively harming your case.

TACTICAL INFORMATION

Everything you do in preparation for trial and during trial ultimately is calculated to make your position as persuasive to the court as possible.

Instead, you and your lawyer will present at trial all the facts that you conclude are useful in constructing the brick wall discussed earlier, which brings me to your next task. To prevail at trial, you must do more than simply locate and deliver to the court your best information. To continue the metaphor, the bricks in your wall must be solid, sturdy bricks. This point concerns your most fundamental goal at trial, namely your desire to persuade. You cannot lose sight of that target. Everything you do in preparation for trial and during trial ultimately is calculated to make your position as persuasive to the court as possible.

Logically, this point raises the following question: how then, do you make your position most persuasive to the court? You will recall, from the earlier discussion regarding discovery, the importance to your case of gathering helpful facts. We discussed the necessity of focusing your most helpful evidence during the trial, with the time permitted to you, but this raises the following question: how do you determine if a fact is helpful, and if so, to what extent it helps? Clearly, any fact that logically or otherwise advances your position in the judge's mind could fairly be termed a helpful fact.

On the other hand, one could also say that helpfulness is determined by the criteria spelled out in the applicable law. It is the legal system's intention that both of these definitions be true simultaneously.

The judge's mind (at least in theory) is in part guided by the applicable law, be it case law or statute. For our purposes, the applicable law is that regarding custody, which comprises a handful of statutes and a multitude of cases. The resultant custody criteria will be discussed at length in another chapter.

Therefore, at the risk of seeming simplistic, your task is to marshal facts that persuade the court that the order you are requesting is exactly what the law dictates in your circumstances. I should add, however, that in practice the definition of what is persuasive is not quite as academic as it sounds. Regarding the governing law, as mentioned elsewhere in this book, it comprises primarily a single statute that contains a handful of amorphous guidelines. These guidelines are interpreted by a large, sundry body of often inconsistent and, as to a given case, inapplicable appellate opinions. The practical effect of this situation is that it effectively delegates very broad discretion to the trial judge, so broad that he can decide whether many facts, even if believable, are consistent or inconsistent with the law without fear of reversal by an appellate court. Sound too subjective? Wait, there's more. The trial judge is also given the right to determine whether a fact is, in fact, a fact. By this I refer to the appellate court's long-standing policy that they will defer (absent clear abuse) to the trial judge's conclusions regarding the credibility or weight to be given to each piece of evidence at trial.

Now let us return to the question of what is persuasive. The answer should be a combination of both sets of concerns where compatible. You must prepare your case and present your evidence with an eye to the law as you best understand it. In addition, you must incorporate into your case evidence that will be most persuasive to the court regarding your position, as long as it is ethical. If, however, there is a contradiction, you have to decide whether the judge's position is so far out of line as to be reversible on appeal, as well as whether an appeal is feasible. Doubtlessly other considerations might come into play as well. At such a juncture, I do not believe there is a single formulaic answer for every case.

Once you determine which facts you want to place into evidence at trial, you then have to ensure that these facts are admissible according to the rules of evidence, which dictate what gets into evidence and how. These rules can be very complex and are often the source of many objections at trial. If the evidence you offer fails to comply, the other attorney will normally object, the court will sustain the objection, and the evidence will not get "on the record," which means the offered evidence, if the case were appealed, will not be considered by the Court of Appeals (absent an offer of proof, which I will not get into here). Additionally, if the objection is sustained, the evidence offered is not to be considered by the trial judge in his decision, even though, as a practical matter, he will often hear and see the evidence. This is another example of what the legal system calls a "fiction" while simultaneously insisting it is real.

Evidence during a trial is entered by one of several court-approved means. I think it will be helpful to you to be familiar with the most important of these, and therefore they are described briefly below.

1. Testimony. This is the type of evidence most people automatically think of when you mention a trial. Television dramas have doubtlessly contributed to the popular

misconception that trial testimony is by nature dramatic, intense, and always entertaining. The reality is quite the opposite. This is attributable in part to the fact that the circumstances underlying most trials, even custody trials, are comparatively mundane to the average layman. Additionally, the rigorous discovery process now routinely used in custody fights and other serious litigation often precludes those otherwise truly suspenseful moments. Also, relentless, staccato cross-examination, for which television dramas are notable, could in reality have been interrupted repeatedly by a variety of valid objections. The fact is that the rules of civil procedure, while giving some latitude to cross-examination, will not tolerate disorder or incivility in the courts. Also, be aware that the term "testimony" may include statements made outside court by witnesses testifying under oath, as in a deposition.

2. Documents. A document for purposes of the evidence rules includes virtually every writing of significance in a case. A writing is defined to include potentially virtually every written communication relating to a given case, whether handwritten, typed, faxed, e-mailed, or drawn. Also, the term has expanded to include any electronic information. As you might guess, documents often play a key role in custody matters. The examples are so varied and numerous that it is difficult to identify a single set of core documents that are consistently used as exhibits in all, or even most, custody proceedings. The documents most commonly seen in such cases are:
    - Employment records of each parent. This would, of course, include W-2 forms and other income information but also relevant may be records relating to historical and even

anticipated work schedules or job transfers, for example.

- Education records of the children.
- Health care records of the children.
- Health care records of one or both of the parents. This is not routine, but may be triggered by a specific allegation. Note that this information may be privileged or otherwise protected by law from use by the opposing party.
- Criminal and other official public records relating to one or both parties. An easy example is police records used to reveal offenses, such as DWI, assault, or other incriminating conduct by a party. There are innumerable other documents potentially relevant to a custody dispute. As suggested above, the issue for you and your attorney is to determine what documents will assist your particular set of facts.

3. Demonstrative exhibits. This category is technically not evidence itself, but it refers to a means of presenting evidence that can be very helpful in custody fights and other litigation. You might call such things visual aids. Demonstrative exhibits may take the form of graphs, charts, and models. The purpose is simply to make the evidence more comprehensible. In court, as in schools and other circumstances where the objective is to teach or explain, this end is often best achieved by making the point visually. This is particularly true of evidence that is otherwise boring, technical, and/or confusing. I will not even try to anticipate here the potential use you may have for demonstrative exhibits in your case. That is your attorney's job. However, the use that I most commonly make of such exhibits is to summarize and give life to detailed information regarding the historical role each parent has had in a child's life. Usually, the underlying data comes from a combination of

sources, such as journals, school records, employment records, or the memories of witnesses. For example, if I want to give the judge a clear understanding of the care-giving schedule of the parents over the preceding five years, I will provide to the court a simple visual aid, such as a bar graph, a calendar, or a pie chart. These are typically color-coded as well. The effect is that I communicate to the judge an essential point in an immediately comprehensible and memorable way. This chart may be as small as 8.5 x 11 inches or as large as a three foot poster. I will add an evidentiary caveat. The underlying evidence must be admissible and placed into evidence, and the visual aid must accurately reflect this evidence. Your attorney must carefully lay this "foundation" to successfully stave off an objection. Also, even though the aid is normally identified and marked as an exhibit, it is not admitted into evidence because, as mentioned above, it is not in itself evidence. My point in mentioning demonstrative exhibits is to stimulate you (with your attorney's guidance) to think creatively about your case. Remember that your case, while infinitely interesting to you, is potentially very dry to a seasoned, perhaps over-seasoned, family court judge.

4. Tangible items. As the name suggests, this type of evidence refers to physical objects or three-dimensional items that in some way become relevant to a legal proceeding. Although this discussion would be incomplete without mention of this type of evidence, I have to confess that although I struggle to remember a single recurrent example of such evidence used in custody disputes, none comes to mind. As a result, I am reduced to the following hypothetical. During the course of a custody dispute, Dad accuses Mom of domestic violence. He cites in support thereof an incident in which she struck

> him over the head with a bookend. If the bookend used was a large, brass, sharply angled figurine, Dad would likely want to introduce the actual figurine into evidence. The opportunity to see and hold it will communicate to the court a capacity for violence that would likely not be fully appreciated on the basis of simple testimony. I will just mention that there are a number of specific evidentiary steps required for admission of such tangible evidence. In any case, it is your lawyer's job to worry about such details.

In a custody dispute, you will likely primarily rely on oral testimony by various people with first-hand knowledge, as well as that of one or more experts. Documents are also typically important, e.g., school and health records. This subject will be discussed further in Chapter 9.

During the trial itself, you and your attorney will be seated together (usually at your own table), as will your wife and her attorney. Many times clients envision a courtroom full of onlookers, as on television. Divorces, unless you are rich and famous, do not command much public interest. Often, apart from the parties and their attorneys, only the judge, a court reporter, and a bailiff are present. Witnesses may or may not be present. Some states may require closed hearings under certain circumstances where minors are involved. Also, witnesses will be excluded if the court grants a motion by either party.

Procedurally, the petitioner must put her case on first. This means she calls her witnesses and presents her exhibits first. Of course, your attorney can cross-examine her witnesses and object at any point to her evidence. If the objection is sustained, the information is not admitted, which means, theoretically, that the judge will not consider it in his eventual decision.

After your wife finishes presenting her case (after she "rests"), you will then present yours. After you rest, the court may permit the petitioner to present "rebuttal" testimony. If so, your wife is limited to evidence refuting your evidence, typically the testimony of one or more of your witnesses. The purpose of rebuttal, as the name implies, is simply to give the petitioner a chance to respond to the respondent's evidence. Thereafter, the trial is concluded.

TACTICAL INFORMATION

8

While opening and closing arguments are permitted in divorce proceedings, most lawyers do not use them.

You may be wondering when those dramatic and mesmerizing opening and closing arguments come in, as you have seen on television. Although it is true that opening and closing arguments are permitted in divorce proceedings as in any other trial, most lawyers do not use them in most cases. Perhaps this is due in part to the fact that in a divorce proceeding you do not have the benefit (or burden) of a credulous and malleable jury. Instead, you have a battle-hardened and sophisticated judge deciding your case. Additionally, and related to the above point, opening and closing arguments are often used to simplify and summarize complex or voluminous evidence. Usually the evidence in divorces is not that voluminous or complex. Furthermore, even when it is, an experienced divorce court judge probably does not need the assistance and may in fact be annoyed by it.

Nonetheless, having said all of the above, I will usually make a closing argument if I sense the judge is unclear as to my client's objectives or an important bit of evidence. Often this is the case when a trial is broken up into segments over several days or when there is a lot of ambiguity in the evidence.

The very idea of a trial, when first discussed with clients, normally triggers anxiety and dread. I believe this is primarily because it seems such a grave and arcane thing to the outsider, whose familiarity with the process is that of an American moviegoer.

Once explained, however, as in this and subsequent chapters, the event can be understood for what it is. Suddenly, it seems less mysterious and, as a result, less intimidating. However, familiarity does more than simply reduce your anxiety. Most importantly, it better equips you to assist in building your case.

7

The Rules of Engagement: The Custody Conundrum

He who knows when he can fight
and when he cannot will be victorious.

-Sun Tzu,
The Art of War,
circa 2000 BC

Count the Cost before the First Shot

Even without children, divorce is a horrendous experience for both parties. The grief is typically greater for the spouse who does not want the divorce. However, the stress and conflict escalate exponentially where children are involved. Kids are the ultimate victims of divorce. Through no fault of their own, their world is turned upside down, and their lives are dramatically and irreversibly changed.

Children of intact homes come to believe in a home-centered universe. Then divorce, like the horsemen of the apocalypse, comes charging through their world. Suddenly the laws of nature they took for granted are suspended. They discover that the entity they viewed singularly, their parents, is sharply and determinably divisible. On top of this psychological welter is heaped bitter, angry, and destructive conflict. Now, in the void between Mom and Dad stands the child. He or she often must choose between them or move forward alone, distanced from both parents by the desire to be left out of their fight.

I apologize if this picture seems unduly bleak. Certainly, there are exceptions. Divorces do occur after which the parents continue to parent cooperatively and jointly. You may know someone for whom this is true. Yet as a veteran of a thousand divorces (directly or indirectly), I can tell you these cases are not the norm. The fact is that no soil is more fertile for conflict than that of estranged lovers linked by the need to raise a child. This almost inevitable conflict, both during and after divorce, bleeds easily into the parent-child relationship. Dad resents Mom's ready willingness to discard the marriage. Mom resents Dad's infidelity. Dad resents having to pay Mom so much money. Mom resents Dad for having so much money. Such resentments tend to find expression in alienating conduct by one or both parents through the child.

Divorced Dad's Tip:

"Custody" is a particularly bad term when discussing children in a divorce. It is used almost in the same manner as gaining custody of the dining room set or the pickup truck. It is a curiosity that two people will fight for the right to care for and protect innocent children by subjecting them to terrible experiences in a courtroom. You may in fact wonder if the people from the 1900s were onto something by "staying together for the children." With divorce now more common than lifelong marriage, today's society exhibits the consequences of aggressive divorce: high rates of children in counseling, the use of medication to treat their behavioral issues, high rates of antisocial behavior and obesity among children. Perhaps after meditating upon the possible long-term negative affects of divorce on children, parents will consider involving a counselor or mediator to take some of the sting out of their children's experience.

It is against this backdrop that you must count the cost. You are in a position now to dramatically affect the rest of your child's life. You stand at a fork in the road. You must decide rationally and dispassionately among the alternatives available to you. This means considering your course in the broad context of things, always acting in your child's best interest.

Dads on the threshold of divorce, like commanders in battle, deal with lives other than their own. The innocent and trusting who must rely on their wisdom are the ones most directly affected by this fervor. What is wisdom at such a crucial juncture? It is in part a careful analysis of your probabilities of getting more than is presently offered to you. You will primarily rely on your attorney's forecast. If you have retained an experienced domestic relations attorney, he will be attuned to the nuances of your case and can give you advice, but apart from the simple mathematics of success, do not forget to consider the cost associated with both winning and losing.

In civil wars, more than in other types of war, a lot of blood is spilt, goodwill vanishes, wounds are inflicted that do not heal, and economic costs often devastate both nations and parents. Naturally, if you lose, the victor is likely to retaliate at every turn in the distant future. Your challenge, where you stand, is to do the heroic. In the face of the ultimate wrong, betrayal by the person you most loved and trusted, you must extricate yourself from this maelstrom of emotion and do the right thing for your kids. This means not only compartmentalizing your feelings toward your wife but also rejecting the gratuitous and insightful urging of friends and family.

If you engage in this deliberative analysis early on before you set your course and then resort to it regularly during the process, you will never have to condemn yourself at the end of the day, whatever the outcome.

What Exactly are you Fighting for?

> Know the enemy
> and know yourself.
>
> *-Sun Tzu,*
> *The Art of War,*
> *circa 2000 BC*

Before you can reach any conclusions as to how you should proceed, you need to know exactly of what victory or failure consists. Obviously, it will pertain to you and your wife's level of participation in your child's life. Legally, this participation is divided into two categories: legal custody and physical custody.

Legal Custody

Legal custody pertains to the authority to make decisions respecting the health, education, and welfare of your children. There are basically three possibilities: sole legal custody to Dad, sole legal custody to Mom, or legal custody to Dad and Mom jointly.

Divorced Dad's Tip:

There are two types of custody: physical and legal. Either may be joint or sole. In many cases the label of sole custody whether legal or physical, incites parents to become defensive and reject the custody proposal. For example, a woman may feel that no self-respecting mother would allow her husband to have "sole physical custody" of her children. She must be a bad mother, a drunk, or a junkie to consent to such a label. The same feelings arise for men. When trying to iron out a custody arrangement, divorcing dads should focus less on these labels and more on the actual schedule. The mother may be labeled as having sole physical custody but you may still have the children fifty percent of the time.

As may be apparent, the notion of joint authority regarding such major decisions has more theoretical than practical appeal. Essentially, you are left with a democracy of two. Nonetheless, virtually every client who comes into my office (if not pursuing sole legal custody) is amazed that the court does not reflexively and routinely award joint legal custody in divorce. I have to admit that there is certainly a favorable appeal to the concept of two parents equally sharing the child-rearing authority. However, the application of the concept quickly exposes the flaws.

As I have previously stated, divorce, by its nature, is unfriendly. Any exceptions you may know serve to prove the rule. The fact is that at least one party, and often just one party, is being left and feels betrayed and exploited, whereas the other party is taking what she can and moving on to a better deal. The resulting conflicts, some substantive and many not, cannot be contained as might a fire on a ship. It is nonsensical to conclude that either, or much less both, of these parents can exercise such Herculean rationality as to compartmentalize issues respecting their children while a scorched-earth strategy is being waged in all other areas.

The fact is that the bitterness and disagreement present at the conclusion of the divorce does not evaporate like spilled milk. More often than not, it further corrodes the relationship as lifestyles change and each parent finds other mates. This is the milieu from which is to emerge, theoretically, a cooperative and productive co-parenting arrangement.

As you might expect, many judges and lawyers, hard-bitten by experience, view the concept of joint legal custody skeptically. In practice, joint legal custody would mean that the parents are capable of agreeing on issues such as schools, extracurricular activities, health care providers, health care, and place of worship and other religious matters. I agree this is a tall order. If I represent a Dad in pursuit of primary physical custody, I discourage him from entering into a joint legal custody arrangement unless it will settle an otherwise shaky case. If, on the other hand, our case for primary physical custody is strong, I caution my client that he should avoid joint legal custody.

Despite its practical limitations, however, joint legal custody does give the noncustodial parent substantially greater leverage than he would otherwise have. By exercising his veto power, he can put the brakes on unilateral decisions Mom may be inclined to make respecting major issues. Furthermore, he has the threat of an action for contempt with which to extract cooperation not otherwise forthcoming. Additionally, if the primary custodian shows a repeated disregard for the court's allocation of parenting authority, the court may, and with increasing frequency does, transfer custody.

As a result, if my client is not likely to obtain primary physical custody, I strongly encourage him to seek joint legal custody. In the absence of primary physical custody, joint legal custody becomes an important mechanism to prevent Mom from reducing Dad to a child support provider and occasional weekend babysitter.

Physical Custody

Regarding physical custody, usually the terminology of "primary" versus "temporary" is used, although increasingly the legislatures and courts have shown a preference for the phrase "joint custody" and a corresponding distaste for the phrase "sole custody."

Most non-lawyers understand, in at least general terms, the typical primary versus temporary arrangement (every other weekend, one evening every week, two to six weeks in the summer, and alternating holidays). However, there are a variety of common revisions to the above schedule that may increase its attractiveness to the noncustodial parent.

The phrase "joint custody," as it pertains to physical custody, is too amorphous to define; its significance is probably more rhetorical than anything else is. It is easier to say what it does not mean. It does not denote a 50/50 allocation of time between parents, no matter what an English language student may be inclined to think. "Joint custody" may, in fact, refer to a schedule in which one parent receives time that is anywhere along the spectrum of 1 percent to 99 percent. The word "joint" simply denotes either a schedule agreed to by the parties, or a plan that the court or legislature has chosen to characterize as "joint."

Defining Your Custody Goals

Most jurisdictions have a standard custodial or parenting plan addressing both legal and physical custody. A copy of the form adopted by St. Louis County, Missouri, can be found in Appendix 4. Note that it specifically covers almost every issue relating to the child. As one judge put it, such documents are "jerk-driven." The judge meant that the original document was short and simple; much of the verbiage owes itself to various "gotchas" perpetrated by one party or the other over time.

Irrespective of whether your jurisdiction has a preprinted form, at a minimum it has a de facto practice respecting physical and legal custody. A court system cannot make its way through 10,000 divorces and greet the next one as if it were a brand-new action unrelated to what has gone before. Over time, patterns emerge, habits and attitudes form in response, and in time, those patterns calcify. This is a system-wide phenomenon. Judges, lawyers, clerks, and social workers all view your divorce through the lenses of their experience.

They are heavily influenced by stereotypes. This institutional prejudice expresses itself in, among other things, the development of standardized parenting plans. In fairness, a subsidiary factor driving judicial systems in the formation of such plans is fatigue. Courts are unable or unwilling to devote the resources necessary to afford every parent a customized divorce. Administrators argue that such an individualized approach is economically impractical. Additionally, it should not go unmentioned that typically, one party to every divorce is quite pleased with the generic product; you might say they end up with the bigger half of justice.

The bottom line is that systemic inertia will press you to accept one of the preprinted roles. You must, pursuant to Missouri's plan, be parent A or B. Although the Missouri form does suggest that you may check a box and use a different plan, to do so is to swim upstream. Remember, your wife will probably welcome the form, assuming she will be parent A.

This brings us to a difficult juncture in the divorce process: do you go for primary custody, 50/50 custody, or temporary custody? These are essentially your three options. Let us consider each in turn.

Regarding 50/50 custody, I have already given a number of very compelling reasons for not choosing one of the two conventional roles courts assign to parents. I would add, however, that a large body of professional literature exists that assumes that children need a primary residence (a home base) for optimal emotional health. Rather than debate the merit of this position, suffice it to say that if you go to trial seeking a 50/50 arrangement, expect to do battle with various experts critical of your position.

That is not to say, however, that you cannot win such a battle. I have fought and won them despite opposing expert testimony, but it is nonetheless a difficult battle. It should be noted that there have been several very influential studies that speak approvingly of 50/50 custody arrangements; among them is a study by Judith Wallerstein.

These studies, however, do not give unqualified approval of such plans. Rather, they argue that where certain elements are present, 50/50 custody can be a good thing. Three of the elements mentioned are as follows:

1. Age of the children. Kids over age five years deal much better with this plan than infants and toddlers.
2. Geographical proximity of the parents. Obviously, exchanges

are more practical if Dad lives one instead of 30 miles from Mom.

3. Low levels of conflict between parents. True cooperation is more practical where parents can cooperate and communicate.

In the early stages of a divorce, when clients and their attorneys are strategizing regarding custody, I always discuss the potential for a 50/50 order. Many men find themselves without a realistic shot at primary custody, not necessarily as a result of discrimination (as discussed below), and are therefore torn between the two general remaining possibilities of 50/50 custody or the more traditional noncustodial schedule. There are of course, an infinite number of gradations in between, but for analytical purposes, it is simpler to view these as discrete categories.

Before I can, in good faith, suggest that a client seriously pursue 50/50 custody (meaning a large investment of time, emotion, and money), there must be exceptional circumstances militating in favor of this arrangement. I would first want to know whether we have a judge who will fairly consider this option. If not, the best of arguments and evidence will fail. Next, I would want a historical record (discussed more fully below) compatible with a true co-parenting arrangement. Additionally, the logistics, for instance, the proximity of the parties' homes and employment and the compatibility of work and other schedules, must come together. Finally, the relationship between the parties must be good. In fact, it is particularly helpful if, during the separation, the parties actually implement such a plan and it works, i.e., the kids appear to benefit from the arrangement. In situations with older children (adolescents or teens), it is important that the children be on board.

The bottom line is that a fight for 50/50 custody should only be undertaken if there are special factors present. Generally speaking, it is a tough row to hoe.

Having dealt with the 50/50 question, let us now consider the alternatives. For explanatory purposes, we will discuss only two: primary to Mom with balance to Dad or primary to Dad with balance to Mom.

Before discussing the criteria the court will use in deciding this question, you must first decide on your goals. This is not the superficial comment that it appears to be because you must ask yourself—setting all anger and bitterness aside—what you really want.

Every time a client sits down in my office and I ask this question without emphasis or explanation, his reflexive answer is always that he wants primary custody. As a result, I have found that it is more helpful to phrase the question as follows: who do you believe your children should live with primarily, given the children's preferences and you and your wife's circumstances going into the future?

This gets to the heart of the matter. Too often, a dad believes the underlying issue is whether he loves his kids. In reality, the question

Divorced Dad's Tip:

It can be hard to focus on your job and visitation with the kids, while plodding through the divorce process. One of the best things you can do to positively affect your custody arrangement is purposefully create your new world around your children. If you get a one-bedroom apartment, where will the kids sleep? Do you have more than one child? Are they different genders? What kind of privacy will they need? It may cost more money for a two-bedroom place, but it's better for your kids. Are you getting a place close to your work, but it's an hour drive from their school or sports fields? Why not get a place closer to the children's school, even though it means adding 30 minutes to your commute? Want to be a big part of your children's lives? Demonstrate to the judge your willingness to make (sometimes inconvenient or even costly) decisions that benefit them.

is a practical one. Where will Dad live in relation to Mom?

Naturally, if Dad plans to live in an apartment or an unfavorable school district and Mom lives in the marital home, which is located in the kids' present school system, that is a factor to be considered. If Dad works 60 hours per week (voluntarily or not) or if he must travel every week while Mom works a straight 9-to-5 schedule, that is a factor to be considered.

It is not a demonstration of a paternal character defect if Mom in fact does most of the hands-on parenting and seems to enjoy it, while Dad has acted primarily as a provider, a role he has chosen and enjoyed. That is not to say that these roles are always cast in stone. New circumstances associated with the divorce could reasonably persuade Dad that these roles must be dramatically altered. Mom may have developed an alcohol problem, she may insist on cohabiting with an unacceptable lover, or she may demonstrate an inalterable determination to extricate the children from Dad. Absent such new and important facts, however, if Ward Cleaver chooses to fight June for primary custody, he needs to have defensible and rational reasons for doing so.

Criteria of the Courts: How You Will Be Judged

After the agonizing decision as to what you consider the best custody arrangement given the fact of divorce, you next must decide whether that preferred scenario is achievable. That brings us to a discussion of the factors that courts consider in reaching their conclusions about custody. When I discuss these items with clients, they are frequently a little surprised that the list is so commonsensical. The facts that a court considers in making its decision are probably the same facts you would list if you wore the black robe.

Custody battles are street fights and not abstract discussions. The issues are pragmatic, and the effects are real. Although experts, such as psychologists, education experts, and physicians, do play important roles, usually the outcome can be predicted by a sort of common-sense tangible analysis, for instance, past parenting role, child's preferences, and work schedules.

To make this discussion more comprehensible, it is helpful to view the relevant evidence as falling into one of four categories: (1) historical picture; (2) prospective picture; (3) status concerns; and (4) child preferences.

The historical picture examines each parent's role in nurturing the child since birth. The following is a list of activities that one could argue constitute the nuts and bolts of child-rearing. As you review each item on this list, assign a percentage to you, your wife, and any third parties who performed that task.

- Getting the child up in the morning
- Getting the child dressed
- Preparing breakfast
- Taking the child to school
- Caring for the child during the daytime
- Preparing lunch
- Picking the child up from school
- Preparing dinner
- Caring for the child in the evening
- Bathing
- Playing with the child in the evening
- Assistance with homework
- Taking the child to the doctor
- Attendance at school functions
- Interaction with teachers
- Attendance at extracurricular events

Complete a separate list for each child if the percentages vary from child to child. Also, separate lists may need to be prepared for several time periods between which the roles may have changed dramatically. For example, mom may have been a homemaker for the first two years of your son's life and then worked full-time thereafter. A single percentage for the child would be misleading if Mom and Dad have been on a largely 50/50 basis since Mom returned to work.

I do not contend that the above list is complete, and furthermore, some of the categories overlap. However, it does provide a fairly good picture of what a court considers as it views the parties' prior arrangements.

As mentioned above, present and future circumstances may make the past marital arrangement impractical. Nonetheless, it is not unfair for a judge to give the past some weight in determining the nature of the future arrangement. I often point out to my clients that a judge is not being sexist or punitive if he says to the man whose wife was a homemaker for ten years, "Why was that arrangement preferable then, but not now?"

The fact that a divorce is in progress obviously is not a sufficient reason in and of itself to, pardon the phrase, transfer primary custody. I often have to assume the role of devil's advocate to vividly communicate important points to my clients. Although the arguments are rarely greeted warmly, they nonetheless better equip my client to testify, as well as to make informed decisions along the way.

As to the prospective picture, regardless of what has been done in the past, sometimes new circumstances require change. Therefore, to make a sound decision regarding custody, the court must consider the parents' respective situations going into the future.

The following is a list of factors that are influential in this respect:

1. Schools. Is one parent going to remain in the same school district that the children presently attend? If so, that is generally helpful. Conversely, is one parent going to have

access to a school substantially superior to the school available to the other parent?

2. Employment. Courts prefer predictable work schedules that are compatible with the children's school and sleep schedules. A work schedule requiring fewer hours is better than one requiring more (including commuting time), more job stability is better than less, and jobs with a lower risk of transfer are preferred. Work-time flexibility is certainly a plus.

3. Residence. Generally speaking, the court prefers good neighborhoods to bad, permanence to transience, houses to apartments, proximity to school and work over distance therefrom, ownership to renting (again more predictability), and large quarters to small quarters.

Other prospective circumstances can come into play. The presence of half-siblings or even step-siblings may be a factor if there is a close relationship with your marital kids. Courts prefer to keep sibling relationships intact.

TACTICAL INFORMATION

The presence of half-siblings or even step-siblings may be a factor in custody determination.

9

A boyfriend or girlfriend may affect the court's prospective analysis if it is believed they will be cohabiting (with or without marriage) with one of the parties. It only makes sense that in weighing the relative circumstances of the parties, the court would consider a third party intending to reside with either spouse.

I have listed here the prospective factors most commonly influencing custody. There are obviously innumerable additional issues that could be powerful in a given case. Most cases have their unique concerns. As you extrapolate from the above to your situation, keep in mind the underlying thread that runs throughout this chapter: custody battles are exercises in common sense.

The third category of factors that determines the outcome of custody battles is status: it relates more to who a parent is than to their past or future conduct. Naturally, determining who someone is often becomes a conclusion based on past behavior, and its relevance relates to anticipated future behavior. Therefore, one could argue that this section is logically contained in the two previous sections. Nonetheless, it is helpful to consider these factors distinctly from the previous ones.

What do I mean by status? Some examples are as follows: male, female, heterosexual, homosexual, schizophrenic, depressive, alcoholic, angry, violent, and sexually perverted.

As I use the term "status," I am really referring to personality or behavioral traits. Most of these have shorthand labels that denote a cluster of characteristics. These characteristics may make or break a custody battle, irrespective of apparently good historical and prospective evidence. For example, evidence of closet drug addiction or a consuming sexual addiction would probably prove determinative of custody. One of the most common status issues that I see relates to alcoholism, either by my client, his spouse, or both.

If a parent has a problem, you can be sure the other parent will point a finger. If my client is accused, I will sit down with him and attempt to determine what objective evidence exists. Has it affected employment? Has he had any criminal incidents? What about a charge of driving while under the influence of some substance (DUI)? Any violence while drinking? If the answer is no to all of these, there is a good chance that we can dodge the bullet.

For example, I represented a dad in his late twenties in a custody battle in which he was accused of alcoholism. He had been hospitalized for drug and alcohol addiction in his teens and had several DUIs, although none within the past three years. My client admitted under cross-examination that he had a drinking problem and that he still drank, but he denied that he presently drank excessively. The court awarded him primary custody and specifically stated in its order that although my client had a history of alcoholism, no evidence was presented to suggest it was presently a problem in his life.

Another common accusation relates to psychological problems. Typically, one parent will allege that the other is not equipped mentally to be a primary custodian. I should mention here that a psychiatric history, in and of itself, does not carry the weight it may have in the past. Forty years ago, evidence of such treatment was stigmatizing. However, in recent years the readiness with which people seek psychological care has diluted its adverse effect, thereby reducing its weight in custody disputes. As I commonly caution clients, the judge's wife (or husband) probably takes Prozac. In and of itself, the fact that a spouse takes an antidepressant or other such medication carries little weight without accompanying significant negative behavior.

Divorced Dad's Tip:

During the divorce, is your spouse continually taking cheap shots at you in front of the children? "We can't go out to the movies because daddy doesn't give us enough money," or "I don't know why your father doesn't come to your swimming matches. I guess his work must be very important to him." These subtle (and not so subtle) mind games are standard fare for some women. Most of the time you have no idea it's happening because it takes place completely out of your sight. Some women vent their rage in front of the children in a manner that undermines their relationship with their father. As a result the children become confrontational, lose respect for their father, and feel a sense of worthlessness and despair. If you see changes in your children's demeanor, perhaps subtle at first, you may wish to speak with your spouse in an effort to stop the badmouthing. Just as important, be sure to curb your own anger in response.

TACTICAL INFORMATION 10

Studies show that women are more likely to engage in Parental Alienation Syndrome.

Finally, there is the subject of alienation. Psychologists call it "Parental Alienation Syndrome." Psychiatrist Richard Gardner, a leading authority who has done a great deal of research in this field, defines it as "a disturbance in which children are preoccupied with deprecation and criticism of a parent-denigration that is unjustified and/or exaggerated."[1] In other words, one parent, by acts or words in the presence of the child, undermines the child's relationship with the other parent.

Gardner points to some of the ways this occurs. The first and perhaps most damaging is "brainwashing," which he describes as "conscious acts of programming the child against the other parent." He says that the alienating parent "embarks upon an unrelenting campaign of denigration...at times the criticism may even be delusional."

Gardner points out that women are more likely to alienate than are men. He attributes this in part to a sense by Mom that she is losing control over the kids. She will complain that Dad does not provide financial support. She will exaggerate minor shortcomings, such as Dad's occasional use of alcohol or his inability to attend a given school event. Gardner further states that moms will often use sarcasm to achieve their goal. "After all these years," she will say, "he's finally gotten around to taking you to a ball game."[2]

Sometimes Mom's efforts are more subtle, and the criticisms are less direct. "There are things I could say about your father that would make your hair stand on end, but I am not the kind of person who criticizes a parent to his children."[3]

Regarding temporary custody, Mom may say, "You have to go see

[1] **Richard Gardner, *Family Evaluation and Child Custody, Mediation, Arbitration and Litigation* (1989) 226.**
[2] **Kare and Ackerman 144.**

your father. If you don't he will take us to court."[4]

Mom will prioritize all the kids' activities ahead of time with Dad. She will interfere with phone contacts by saying the kids are eating or doing their homework.[5]

The process becomes a vicious circle in which Dad becomes increasingly insistent about communication and time with his kids, and Mom accuses him of harassing her.

The impulse often seems irresistible; in the spousal war of words, extra points, it would seem, are awarded for jibes delivered in the presence of the kids. The temptation to "expose" Mom to the kids is tantalizing. Mom's infidelity is a particularly disclosure-prone piece of information. On a less titillating level are the numerous occasions on a day-to-day basis when you can control the message you telegraph to your kids regarding your opinion of Mom. My advice is simple: resist!

I realize you are likely to retort that if you resist the urge to badmouth Mom, you are fighting by Marquis of Queensbury rules, while your wife is using the tactics of a street fighter. Nonetheless, I stand by my advice. My position to clients is on two levels. One is strategic, and the other, with which you may not be impressed, is moral.

Regarding strategy, I tend to believe that where a playing field is reasonably flat (as it thankfully is in most jurisdictions), and where you are represented by at least competent counsel, what is true and good tends to distill to the surface during the litigation process. Of course, this is not a natural law without exception, but it is sufficiently probable to guide your conduct in your case.

The second reason is that despite Machiavellian dictum, the ends do not always justify the means. Where your kids are concerned, and where you and another person are the center of their solar system, it is deeply wrong to further destabilize their world. Parental alienation

[3] **Ibid 240.**
[4] **Ibid 223.**
[5] **Ibid 236.**

is far more hurtful than parents realize when they engage in it. I would add that the cliché about fighting fire with fire is a nonsensical statement. You fight fire with water or other substances calculated to arrest it in its tracks. Being able to claim the moral high ground can not only be of tremendous strategic benefit but can also be a means by which to put out the bonfires that preoccupy the lives of the parties, and more importantly the children, involved in a custody dispute. You do not have to like your ex-wife, but treating her with outward respect, particularly in front of the children, can result in a substantial public relations victory and be of benefit to the psychological well-being of your child. Today, courts are increasingly willing to take dramatic preventive steps when persuaded that alienation is occurring. The issue could very well be determinative of custody. Therefore, do not jeopardize your case for a few cathartic moments, however gratifying.

TACTICAL INFORMATION 11

You should never ask your children who they would prefer to live with.

I would be naive however, if I did not add that such conduct is often difficult to prove. Sadly, it is a basic fact of divorce that parents do communicate to kids their grievances with the other parent.

Related to the alienation issue is whether to query the kids regarding whom they prefer to live with. Although it is true that the court may be interested in their opinions, you should never put this question to the kids. There are several ways the court can obtain this information without the kids feeling that they are being asked to choose and without being in the presence of a parent. I would add that despite your confidence in the candor of your child, your child will lie to you. A good rule of thumb is that "I don't know," translates as "Mom," whereas "Dad" translates as "I don't know." The lesson here is simple: do not ask.

The final general category is that of child preference. This subject has to be dealt with carefully to avoid a misimpression. I will begin by saying two things: (1) a child's opinion is virtually always relevant, and (2) a child's opinion is almost never determinative. If you assume all other factors are equal, then a child's preference will typically tilt the scales, but in reality, all other things are never equal. Often other considerations may conflict with the child's preference, and therefore the court has to examine the child's mind set closely to determine what weight it should be given.

The court must first determine whether the child's stated preference is real. You probably would not be shocked to learn that parents often undertake propaganda campaigns during a divorce to win the hearts and minds of their kids. The court has various devices available to it to determine the child's genuine wishes. The court may do an "in camera" interview with the child wherein the judge, the lawyers, or both ask questions of the child in a manner intended to be the least intimidating without the parents present. Additionally, the court may appoint a guardian ad litem, an attorney whose job it is to protect the child's interests.

Finally, many jurisdictions have available social workers or other professionals to conduct, among other things, custody evaluations. Each of these devices will be discussed more fully later.

When discussing child preferences, several factors come into play. First is the age of the child. Clients often ask, "At what age can a child choose?" The technical answer to that question is that he cannot choose until he is either emancipated or reaches age 18 years, but of course, the technical answer is misleading. Although the principle that a child does not have complete autonomy as long as he or she is a child, ie., a minor, makes sense, equally reasonable is the expectation that older kids' opinions should be given serious consideration. I tell clients that a rough rule of thumb is that a child's opinion matters in direct proportion to his or her age, like an upward-sloping curve.

The second factor the court weighs when considering a child's preferences is the reasoning underlying the child's opinion. Are the reasons good? A closer relationship to one parent is understandable, as is a greater willingness to help with school, closer proximity to school and friends, or dislike of an anticipated stepparent. Conversely, if the reason is that the preferred parent does not discipline, has no curfew, or does not enforce homework, then the child's preference will likely be ignored.

Keep in mind that the above general principles are just that, general. They are subject to numerous exceptions and qualifications. Other factors may negate those mentioned. Obviously, it is impossible to include in this discussion all the myriad possibilities that might come into play in a custody battle.

You may be interested to know that psychologists and others have conducted surveys of judges to determine what factors influenced them most in deciding custody battles. In one such survey, 156 judges were asked to rank nine factors in order of importance in their custody decisions.[6] The results were as follows.

- Desires of a 15-year-old child
- Custody investigation report
- Testimony of the parties
- Testimony of a court-appointed psychologist

Also listed, although of less importance, were the following.

- Testimony of school personnel
- Desires of a 10-year-old child
- Testimony of a psychologist retained by one side
- Testimony of extended family members

[6] Reidy, et al, "Child Custody Decisions: a Survey of Judges," ***Family Law Quarterly 23*** **(Spring 1989): 86.**

The judges ranked as least important the desires of a 5-year-old child. These results are consistent with the factors described in my analysis: older kids' opinions are very influential. Items 2, 3, and 4 incorporate or reflect the factors discussed above.

Having pointed out the above considerations affecting a custody battle, I should mention a few factors that generally do not determine custody. I mention these because clients are often surprised, sometimes happily, that these factors do not weigh heavily (if at all) in the court's decision.

The first is adultery. Generally speaking, a court cannot punish a parent for infidelity by denying him or her custody. Furthermore, the court cannot constitutionally base its custody decision on whether a parent is guilty of adultery. In fact, the entire sphere of morality-based decisions as they relate to custody is unclear in the aftermath of American Civil Liberties Union activism. Even homosexuality, once

Divorced Dad's Tip:

There is a predominant theory that a mother invariably will get custody of children (particularly younger children) unless she can be proven unfit – alcoholic, neglectful, mentally ill, drug user, etc. According to the letter of the law, there is no presumption that the mother gets custody of the children. While being able to prove that the mother is unfit will undoubtedly help you obtain custody, it is not absolutely necessary. It is just as important to show why you are a good parent. In many cases either parent could prove a worthy, capable and caring primary custodian. Indeed, in many cases most children would benefit from having as much time with both parents, period. The reason the predominant theory (mothers always get the kids) came into being is because historically the Courts have favored the mother. Do not let this discourage you! Good fathers should have the opportunity to remain very active in their children's lives. The Court should not have the right to reduce your ability to maintain a relationship with your children simply because you are male.

fatal to a parent in a custody battle, is now acceptable, if not actually statutorily blessed, in most states.

Another common fallacy is the belief that Dad, because he earns more money, has an edge over Mom, who may just be entering the job market without skills. At a glance, this disparity seems relevant; the person with more money can give a better standard of living to the child. However, the legislatures have designed child support with just such a possibility in mind. Child support will be discussed in more detail later. Suffice it to say, however, that regardless of the particular scheme adopted by your state, generally speaking, one's child support obligation rises and falls in tandem with his or her income. To summarize this paragraph more bluntly, the court can redistribute the income as is required to adequately (many would say "lavishly") fund the primary custodial parent's needs.

Another common but erroneous assumption regarding custody disputes is that the father, to gain primary custody, has the burden of proving that the mother is unfit. This is nonsense, at least legally. The equal protection clause of the Fourteenth Amendment to the US Constitution, as well as similar provisions adopted by virtually all states, forbids discrimination on the basis of gender.

Although judges cannot lawfully hold men to such a standard in a custody dispute, I would be less than candid if I did not concede that in some jurisdictions and in some courtrooms, the de facto burden is on men in custody disputes. This is particularly true of benighted rural areas, where such prejudices are permitted to flourish. As a practical matter, it is difficult to demonstrate when such wrongs are committed. Seldom does the judge admit such bias.

Discrimination Danger

Every state has on its books laws that forbid discrimination on the basis of gender. Additionally, the Federal Constitution assures all citizens due process and equal protection under the law, but such abstractions are too often ignored in the rough-and-tumble setting of family courtrooms across America day in and day out. Most frustrating perhaps is the difficulty one faces in proving in any given case that such discrimination has occurred. The key players (judges, guardians ad litem, and social workers) are fully aware that in the vast majority of cases they can camouflage such prejudices by clothing their positions in appropriate, but otherwise not determinative, language. Custody disputes, by their nature, involve numerous amorphous factors. As a result, there must be an exceptional disparity between the quality of each parent's case to prove such gender bias.

An additional hurdle to showing such bias is the deference that a court of appeals shows to the trial judges' conclusions about the facts, which will be discussed more fully in a later chapter. Suffice it to say that the trial judge's factual conclusions must be way out in left field to be reversible.

8

Fighting the Fight for Custody: Strategies and Tactics

He who occupies the field
of battle first and awaits his enemy is at ease;
he who comes later to the scene
and rushes into the fight is weary.

-Sun Tzu,
The Art of War,
circa 2000 BC

Having made your way to this chapter, you have examined your custody options, weighed the various factors determining the outcome, and presumably decided on your objective (temporary, joint, or primary custody.)

If your objective is one to which your wife is amenable, you may need to read no further. For example, if you have concluded that realistically, the standard temporary custody schedule discussed previously is most suitable to your situation, you probably will not need to wage war to get there. If, on the other hand, your wife views the children as her separate property, or if she alleges that you have some disqualifying defect, then even to achieve the standard temporary custody schedule, you may have to fight in essentially the same manner as if you were pursuing primary custody.

This chapter focuses on the actual nuts and bolts of waging a custodial war, including the various logistic and strategic considerations that come into play. It is organized in roughly chronological order, although depending on your particular state or jurisdiction, some stages of the process may be reordered.

Custody Issues before Filing: Positioning Yourself Early

Filing a petition is the step that formally launches a dissolution action and triggers the panoply of laws governing divorce. Among these laws are provisions regarding interim custody of children, i.e., laws that spell out who has what custody rights before a court issues an order. These provisions are intended to prevent ugly scrambles before a court has the opportunity to issue a temporary order, which stays in effect until the final order in the divorce proceeding.

It should be noted, however that some states have statutes that address the prefiling period. For example, Missouri recently passed a law that states the following:

> **§ 452.310.3 Upon the filing of the petition in a proceeding for dissolution of marriage or legal separation, each child shall immediately be subject to the jurisdiction of the court in which the proceeding is commenced, unless a proceeding involving allegations of abuse or neglect of the child is pending in juvenile court. Until permitted by order of the court, neither parent shall remove any child from the jurisdiction of the court or from any parent with whom the child has primarily resided for the sixty days immediately preceding the filing of a petition for dissolution of marriage or legal separation.**

This clearly restricts the range of options otherwise available before filing. In the absence of such a statute, you can make a decision as to whether you will file with or without children in your care. In some jurisdictions, this can be a key decision. Many courts refuse to try a custody dispute twice. As a practical matter, what that means is that the court will not hear a full-blown trial over custody at the temporary hearing and then suffer through what would presumably be the same or similar evidence at the final hearing.

Therefore judges have a tendency (absent a Missouri-style statute to the contrary) to maintain the status quo at the temporary hearing and reserve to the final hearing the various issues relating to custody.

Divorced Dad's Tip:

While divorce Courts may historically favor women, ultimately they are no different than regular courts: they look for real evidence. A Judge may be willing to "err on the side of safety" when it comes to an order of protection. However, if a woman cannot prove her allegations, the Court may not grant such an order. The same can be said for the father. Ultimately, your case for custody, visitation, and child support will be based on evidence and facts. The best thing you can do to advance your case is to document as many facts as possible. For example document, every time you take your daughter to soccer, every visit with your son's teacher for PTA meetings, every hour you spend on homework. Nothing speaks louder or affirms a father's claim more unquestionably than a years worth of documentation of time spent with the children. Tell the judge that you are extremely involved in your children's lives; therefore, the Court should insist the relationship continue. The judge will not be able to see this unless you document it. The same is true of disruptions brought on by your wife. Every time she interferes with visitation, sends the kids away for a week during your vacation time, or they come down with a mysterious illness during your time, write it down. Establishing a history of interference will speak volumes to a judge. Your tip of the day: document everything!

Depending on the waiting period for a trial, the interim custodial arrangement could substantially advance or reduce your chances of victory at the final hearing. Often a case remains pending in excess of one year before it actually goes to trial. This affords an opportunity to the interim custodial parent to create a record of exemplary parenting, and indeed for some, it is a necessary period to rehabilitate their image as a parent.

Divorced Dad's Tip:
Most courts will not hear a custody dispute twice. In the beginning stages of your divorce you may have a temporary order in place. It could be months before a hearing on permanent custody is held. If there is a long time between the filing of the original paperwork and the court hearing, this gives you an excellent opportunity to document your relationship with your children and to make life changes that benefit them. Doing so will demonstrate your commitment to your children as well as your willingness to accommodate their needs.

Additionally, the interim parent benefits by creating a somewhat settled status quo going into trial. A judge will likely be substantially influenced by the fact that the child at trial is established in a home, a neighborhood, and a school, assuming, of course, that the child is thriving in that environment.

It should be noted that for dads in particular, there is often a need to prove their ability to be a primary care giver. Moms will often allege that Dad did not in fact provide much assistance during the marriage. I have found this to be true, even when both parents' work schedules during the marriage are comparable.

Obviously even in those jurisdictions that permit it, it is not always practical for Dad to obtain interim primary care. The reasons are varied: (1) Mom may file first, in which case she determines the status quo at the date of filing; (2) there may be no appropriate place for Dad to reside with the children, whereas Mom is still in the home;

and (3) Dad's present work schedule in relation to mom's militates against interim primary custody for Dad.

Keep in mind that the pendency period—the time while the case is pending—provides as much opportunity for loss as for gain. Regardless of the interim custodial arrangement, the parties' conduct during this period will be scrutinized. This will be discussed further below.

If, for logistical or other reasons, you conclude that you cannot obtain interim primary custody, your fallback position must be joint custody (at least a 50/50 arrangement). Unless the parties can reach an interim agreement as to a 50/50 schedule, which at this stage would be exceptional, the optimum arrangement is for Dad to continue living in the marital home throughout the pendency of the case. Furthermore, Dad must seize every opportunity for nurturing his children, and he must document everything.

TACTICAL INFORMATION 12

Dad must seize every opportunity for nurturing his children, and he must document everything.

However, a caveat is in order here if Dad decides to continue living in the home. Virtually every state has its own version of an adult abuse order. This subject is discussed more fully elsewhere. Suffice it to say that these devices are intended to protect the victims of domestic violence. The unfortunate reality, however, is that they are often used as tools for women in divorce. Although nominally gender neutral, the truth on the ground is that men have a heavier burden than women in trying to get such an order issued.

These legal devices consist of two stages. The first is the ex parte order, which issues on the applicant's word alone without the opposing party being given an opportunity to be heard. If an ex parte order is granted, the defendant is ejected from his home with only his personal effects. He is forbidden to return to his home or anywhere else that his wife may be. He also will be deprived of custody of his children, and his access will be narrowly restricted, if not eliminated entirely. He must live this way until stage two, which is the full order hearing. This hearing typically occurs ten to fifteen days (and sometimes up to 30 days) after the ex parte order is issued.

The full order hearing provides this process with a cloak of constitutionality in that it is the theatrical point at which a citizen is afforded his "due process." However, as any experienced lawyer will tell you, the cold reality is that in the vast majority of courts, the hearing is summary in nature, with a presumption against the defendant. The good legislative intentions and the vigilance of constitutional theory are of little assistance to the accused, as he stands in a crowded courtroom in rural Missouri before a judge determined to err on the side of caution. Despite law to the contrary, the reality is that ex parte orders and full orders of protection are casually granted to women in

---

Divorced Dad's Tip:

Should you remain in your home while the divorce proceeds? Every case is different. There are benefits to staying in or moving out of the home. Staying at home allows you to continue a relationship with your children, despite your tenuous relationship with your spouse. If you stay at home for nine months, for example, spending time with your children, your case will be strengthened. The other argument is that staying so close to your wife puts you at a great deal of risk. In more cases than anyone cares to admit, some women abuse the "order of protection" offered by the courts. Often in heated divorces, a desperate or unscrupulous wife will falsely claim abuse or fear of abuse from her husband. He will be removed from the home as if he were guilty, without the benefit of trial; worse, his time with the children will likely be affected. If a Court grants an Order of Protection, your wife will use the Order of Protection against you in the custody battle. So when considering remaining in the marital home, speak to your attorney and give the matter serious thought.

---

many, if not most, courtrooms across America.

With that in mind, any dad choosing to reside in the marital home with his wife while a case is pending assumes some risk. Naturally, the degree of risk varies from case to case. Obviously, having an order of protection issued against you does not help your custody case. Furthermore, in many jurisdictions, it is held against you by statute in matters affecting custody.

In summary, when weighing the option of trying to stay in the marital home, you have to perform a balancing act. On the one hand, consider the opportunities it affords you to continue parenting during the pendency of the case (as discussed above). On the other hand, consider the risk associated with that strategy, as well as your accompanying misery index.

If you opt to attempt to stay in the home with your wife, you must walk on eggshells, bite your lip when baited, and refuse to be drawn into any confrontation. This is easier said than done. I cannot count the number of occasions that clients have vowed to me that they would not be drawn into direct conflict and yet have been. Grand strategy dims in the heat of an argument at 1:00 A.M. Saturday morning. I hear about it when I get to the office Monday morning, and immediately, my client is on the defensive.

If you think you are significantly vulnerable to such manipulation and/or fabrication, I recommend that you consider a strategic retreat. It may make more sense to move from the house voluntarily, taking what property you want and yet aggressively continuing to parent.

From a more panoramic perspective, consider whether a delay in filing your petition is to your benefit or detriment. This, of course, assumes that your wife has not already filed and that you do not anticipate her filing soon. In considering a delay in filing, you have to consider your and your wife's relative positions given the criteria discussed earlier. Then, consider whether an additional six months, for example, would enable you to improve your relative position as a parent, or on the other hand, whether time is your enemy irrespective of your interim efforts. It is possible that a delay could provide a period during which you are aware of what lies around the corner while your wife is not, which may afford you an opportunity to solidify your position as the primary nurturer, as well as to gather information and evidence. Obviously, these opportunities do not exist to the same extent once your wife has been served with a summons. Typically, she will quickly circle the wagons and prepare for battle.

During the Pendency of the Case

You have filed your petition, and your wife has been served (or vice versa). Now consider your next step. The following are some good guidelines to follow while the case is pending.

Discussions With Spouse

My clients often ask me whether they should be negotiating with their spouse. You will probably not be surprised when I say that it depends. If your rapport is such that you are capable of reaching an agreement, I would not discourage discussion as long as you do it in tandem with your attorney. Bear in mind that it can be disastrous if you make concessions or cut deals that it turns out are inadvertently lavish or, conversely, grossly unreasonable. These deals are ultimately deal killers. They create expectations, which then calcify into intractable positions. When someone talks to his lawyer and then announces the deal is off, bad blood results. Even worse, the other party persists in pursuing the putative deal, figuring that the other party is at heart willing to do it despite what his lawyer says. This psychodynamic is a common and real problem in domestic relations. In addition to these practical complications, the litigation fallout from the miscommunication can easily double your attorney's fees.

My clients are, generally speaking, more likely to extract a favorable deal from their wives directly without her counsel than vice versa. The reason is that my clients are often more sophisticated and assertive than their wives, but the deal, as discussed, is illusory. I wish I had a nickel for every occasion a man has sat in my office and naively but emphatically told me that he and his wife have worked out the child-related issues, and the matter is a done deal. Although it is important to preserve a working relationship with your partner in parenting, this does not require you to haggle about your court case. If you are that exceptional couple that can reach a satisfactory agreement through direct negotiations, then do so, being careful to keep the attorneys in the loop.

For the majority of the cases in my office, however, it is a mistake for the clients to negotiate directly, even when I am in the loop. The foremost reason is that there is often no prospect for agreement when you are asking your wife for primary or even joint custody of your kids. Typically, this matter is not open for discussion, either because mom has a visceral proprietary claim to the children and/or because she figures that if she stands firm, the court will, in the end, give her primary custody.

Parenting During Pendency

TACTICAL INFORMATION

A guardian ad litem is the eyes and ears of the judge with regard to custody matters.

13

I have already discussed the importance of an active parenting role while the case is pending. You will recall that strategically you should have a plan before you file regarding your opportunity to parent during the pendency of the case. Obviously, this issue is less important if you go to trial in four months than if you expect to be waiting for two years. Suffice it to say on this subject that you should seize every opportunity presented to you to participate, be it physical, religious, educational, or medical in nature.

Alienation

As already discussed, alienation is a pivotal issue in many divorces. Courts are vigilant for such behavior by either parent while a case is pending. Naturally, we have little control over Mom's behavior. Hopefully, we have control over yours. In short, do not attempt to alienate the children from their mom. It will come out, and the court will punish you for it.

Guardian Ad Litem: Second Front or Ally?

Another important element in a divorce proceeding where custody is at stake is the guardian ad litem. A guardian ad litem is an attorney appointed by the judge to investigate the situation regarding the children and report back to the judge. Depending on individual state's laws, the circumstances under which a guardian ad litem will be appointed vary. Typically, there will be a guardian ad litem appointed if there are allegations of abuse or neglect or if the parties are highly polarized such that the judge wants an independent assessment of the situation.

Although many attorneys and divorce litigants think of the guardian ad litem as the children's attorney, such is not exactly the case. In particular, an attorney must generally follow his client's wishes, whereas the guardian ad litem does not have to do exactly what the children want. Rather, the guardian ad litem is more the eyes and ears of the judge with regard to custody matters, having the power to be present and ask questions at depositions, interview witnesses, draw conclusions, and place those conclusions before the judge. If the guardian ad litem is on your side, it can be a big help in negotiating a favorable custody settlement; conversely, if the guardian ad litem seems to take the other side, it can be a major stumbling block.

The precise nature of a guardian ad litem is the subject of some confusion. The proponents of the guardian ad litem system want to empower the guardian ad litem with all the authority of an attorney in the case without, however, saddling him with the corresponding duties and responsibilities. A guardian ad litem is therefore often clumsily characterized as an "attorney for the child," but when scrutinized further you find that, unlike an attorney in a legal proceeding, many jurisdictions treat him as a court-appointed expert, with the expectation that he will make a recommendation to the court. He is often shielded from malpractice liability and may or may not show up at various depositions during the pendency of the case.

At trial, he is given special treatment procedurally. Because the guardian ad litem is appointed by the court and does not have an importuning client to whom he must answer, the amount of effort he expends in a case is largely up to him.

In fairness, some guardians ad litem devote a great deal of

Divorced Dad's Tip:

Often the Court will appoint a special, unbiased representative (a guardian ad litem) to serve the interest of the children. This person is not acting as an attorney, but as someone who offers opinions to the court – opinions that carry significant weight with most courts. A guardian ad litem is not necessarily a trained counselor or other degreed specialist. Sometimes he or she is just an attorney who has taken a class. Their objective is to listen to the parents, children, teachers and coaches and make recommendations concerning custody. If you are dealing with a guardian ad litem, be truthful and forthcoming. Your objective is to demonstrate that you are a good parent. If your wife makes allegations against you (for example, you are excessively harsh or even violent when disciplining the children), be prepared to respond to the allegations. But beware: the guardian ad litem may not be a clinical or psychological practitioner, only a court representative. If you feel their opinion is based on expediency (the court's interest in avoiding a hearing), consult your attorney to determine if your case will be strengthened by getting an expert (such as a psychologist) to investigate.

attention to their "clients," but others do not. In part this is because guardian ad litem work does not typically pay that well. Courts may limit guardian ad litem fees so that attorneys may simply feel obliged to do the work at a lower hourly rate.

The result is that many, although not all, who pursue this work, do not have particularly successful practices. Furthermore, many are children's rights oriented in perspective, meaning a more interventionist attitude that is less respectful of parental authority. In fact, by definition, one who pursues such a role is betraying a belief that Mom and/or Dad cannot be trusted to know what is best for his or her child, but the guardian ad litem does.

I do not want to poison the well in terms of your perspective toward guardians ad litem. Let me pause here to say that they can be an extremely powerful ally in a custody dispute. They can throw their inflated credibility behind your position and consequently force the other side to settle when the judge announces in a pretrial conference that he is inclined to go with the guardian ad litem's recommendation.

Because the purpose of this book is to educate you about the custody process, I have to occasionally discuss some philosophical issues. This is one of those places. Notwithstanding what I said in the previous paragraph regarding guardians ad litem as potential allies, the disinterested truth, and perhaps your starting inclination, should be that they are neither appropriate nor helpful. A guardian ad litem is often simply an attorney who has taken some classes. The fact is that there is no reason to believe that a guardian ad litem is better equipped than a parent (or anyone else for that matter) to determine what is in a child's best interests. The concept that the position stated by the guardian ad litem constitutes the child's best interests is ridiculous. The travesty is magnified when the child is under the age of five. The fact that the guardian ad litem is a lawyer makes him no more qualified than the proverbial man on the street to say what is best for the child. Exacerbating this fiction is the fact than an otherwise bilateral dispute is now triangular, increasing confusion, time, and fees.

Although I think that the two parents, albeit in a very flawed adversarial process, are capable of bringing to the court the information it needs to reach a decision (including expert opinion), failing this, the court may appoint its own expert, presumably a psychologist, to do an independent evaluation. In contrast to the guardian ad litem, the latter approach has the virtue of at least introducing a competent third party into the process.

The sad reality is that guardians ad litem are used by many judges and attorneys to effectively force settlements in custody disputes, thereby avoiding a trial. Judges in particular are prone to avoid, where possible, the stress, effort, and appellate risk of a trial. By appointing the guardian ad litem, both parties are on notice that "the court's deputy" is appointed with a special standing before the court. The implicit (if not expressed) message is that you never go into trial as the favorite when your position is contrary to that of the guardian ad litem.

Often one or both attorneys will seek a guardian ad litem to avoid having to try the case, even if they suspect the guardian ad litem will oppose their client's position. This is a graceful, if dishonorable, way to sidestep an implacable client's demand for his day in court. "Bill, there's nothing I can do. The guardian ad litem did his investigation and has made his report. I can try the case if you want, but we're on notice as to what the judge is going to do. It's your money." Put differently, the lawyer does not have to take the rap when his client loses because it is the guardian ad litem's fault.

Although many jurisdictions may be predisposed to appoint guardians ad litem for the reasons indicated, the guardian ad litem statutes in many states provide that a guardian ad litem may be appointed at the discretion of the court on motion by either party or on the court's own motion. Where, however, one of the parties alleges "abuse or neglect," the court must appoint a guardian ad litem. Upon the appointment of a guardian ad litem, the court will order one or both parties to put up a deposit with the court for the fees. Often the fees are apportioned on the clients' ability to pay, which typically amounts to a ratio of the respective incomes of the parties.

For purposes of illustration, the following is Missouri's guardian ad litem statute (as of 2007).

> **§ 452.423. 1. In all proceedings for child custody or for dissolution of marriage or legal separation where custody, visitation, or support of a child is a contested issue, the court may appoint a guardian ad litem. The court shall appoint a guardian ad litem in any proceeding in which child abuse or neglect is alleged. Disqualification of a guardian ad litem shall be ordered in any legal proceeding only pursuant to chapter 210, RSMo, or this chapter, upon the filing of a written application by any party within ten days of appointment, or within ten days of August 28, 1998, if the appointment occurs prior to August 28, 1998. Each party shall be entitled to one disqualification of a guardian ad litem in each proceeding, except a party may be entitled to additional disqualifications of a guardian ad litem for good cause shown.**
>
> **2. The guardian ad litem shall:**
>
> **(1) Be the legal representative of the child at the hearing, and may examine, cross-examine, subpoena witnesses and offer testimony;**
>
> **(2) Prior to the hearing, conduct all necessary interviews with persons having contact with or knowledge of the child in order to ascertain the child's wishes, feelings, attachments and attitudes. If appropriate, the child should**

be interviewed;

(3) Request the juvenile officer to cause a petition to be filed in the juvenile division of the circuit court if the guardian ad litem believes the child alleged to be abused or neglected is in danger.

3. The appointing judge shall require the guardian ad litem to faithfully discharge such guardian ad litem's duties, and upon failure to do so shall discharge such guardian ad litem and appoint another. The judge in making appointments pursuant to this section shall give preference to persons who served as guardian ad litem for the child in the earlier proceeding, unless there is a reason on the record for not giving such preference.

4. The guardian ad litem shall be awarded a reasonable fee for such services to be set by the court. The court, in its discretion, may award such fees as a judgment to be paid by any party to the proceedings or from public funds. Such an award of guardian fees shall constitute a final judgment in favor of the guardian ad litem. Such final judgment shall be enforceable against the parties in accordance with chapter 513, RSMo.

5. The court may designate volunteer advocates, who may or may not be attorneys licensed to practice law, to assist in the performance of the guardian ad litem duties for the court. The volunteer advocate shall be provided with all reports relevant to the case made to or by any agency or person and shall have access to all records of such agencies or persons relating to the child or such child's family members. Any such designated person shall receive no compensation from public funds. This shall not preclude reimbursement for reasonable expenses.

Having been rather strident in my opposition to guardians ad litem conceptually, I do concede that in a narrow number of cases, a guardian ad litem may be appropriate. In cases of abuse or neglect where one or both parties have apparently forfeited their parental discretion by such conduct toward the child, a guardian ad litem may be appropriate, but these cases are rare. Even in those cases in which abuse or neglect is alleged, more often than not the accuser is merely mouthing a mantra intended to gain a strategic edge or specifically to trigger the appointment of a guardian ad litem.

Notwithstanding the aforementioned criticisms, a guardian ad litem may end up assisting you in your custody goals. Obviously if the guardian ad litem supports your position, you are glad to have him. The difficult call is when a guardian ad litem is appointed whose position is adverse to yours. Generally, the best policy is to continue to cooperate and cultivate good relations to the extent possible. This is a sort of damage control. Once the guardian ad litem has been appointed, he is irrevocably a factor in the case. You can make the best of it (the more prudent course) or pull up the drawbridge and declare war. Rarely is the latter tactically advantageous. Where a guardian ad litem is demonstrably incompetent or biased, you can move for his removal. This is not, however, a request that is casually granted.

You may be wondering when, if ever, it is advantageous for you to move for the appointment of a guardian ad litem. I can think of several situations where this could be warranted (principles aside).

1. If one of the parties is alleging abuse or neglect, you probably have no alternative per your state statute.
2. If, in your jurisdiction, you have the ability to choose your guardian ad litem or you can identify your guardian ad litem in advance, you may be able to find out if the guardian ad litem is sympathetic to your position on the issues of the case. For example, in one county where I practice, I know the

judge leans toward a particular attorney for his guardian ad litem appointments. I also have a good relationship with that attorney because he is notoriously opinionated, and I can predict with certainty his views on many matters. When my client's position and his views line up, particularly if I am doubtful about the judge's hearings, I may move for the appointment of a guardian ad litem. You are probably wondering how I could be so hypocritical. The fact is that I have a higher duty to my client than to my sociological stance, irrespective of its verity.

Use of Experts

During the course of custody litigation, a professional often becomes involved for purposes of evaluation. In fact, the trend in child custody litigation shows an explosion in the use of expert witnesses since 1920. A prominent study has shown that experts were rarely used in such cases in the first half of this century.[1] By 1995, however, the percentage had risen to 38 percent. I would estimate that in 1999, the percentage has risen to approximately 50 percent. Furthermore, surveys of judges have demonstrated that judges regard expert testimony as very influential in their ultimate decision, particularly when the expert is court appointed.[2]

In General

By definition, a professional involved for evaluation purposes is someone who is not a "treating" professional. It is generally, (or at least increasingly) agreed that a treating professional (a counselor

[1] Mary Ann Mason and Ann Quirk, "Are Mothers Losing Custody? Read My Lips: Trends in Judicial Decision-Making in Custody Disputes—1920, 1960, 1990 and 1995," *Family Law Quarterly 3* (1997).
[2] Ibid 235-236, also "The Wisdom of Solomon: Criteria for Child Custody From the Legal and Clinical Points of view," *Law & Human Behavior 8* (1984): 117.

that the parties may have been seeing) cannot provide an objective evaluation. In fact, the ethical principles of psychologists and a code of conduct of the American Psychological Association expressly disapprove of such a dual role. I use the word "professional" because that person could have any number of occupations. The evaluator could be any of the following:

1. Counselor. This is a very broad term. In most states, this person is licensed, although it may not be required. The result is that a counselor could be anything from a highly qualified professional to a transient and inept opportunist.
2. Social worker. A social worker typically has a masters degree in social work and is employed by a governmental entity. Many county judicial systems have a corps of social workers available for use in custody and other family conflicts.
3. Psychologist. As generally used, this phrase refers to a mental health care professional with a PhD in psychology. This professional is not to be confused with a psychiatrist, as discussed below. Psychologists are far and away the most commonly used experts in custody litigation.[3] Psychologists have completed hundreds of hours of undergraduate and graduate study in the field of psychology and are often members of the American Psychological Association. There are five areas of practice: counseling, school, industrial, experimental, and clinical. Of these, only clinical psychologists are properly trained to do custody evaluations. According to a leading child custody psychologist, to be an

[3] Mary Ann Mason and Ann Quirk, "Are Mothers Losing Custody? Read My Lips: Trends in Judicial Decision-Making in Custody Disputes—1920, 1960, 1990 and 1995," ***Family Law Quarterly 31*** **(Summer 1997).**
[4] Personal communication, Dr. David Clark, 1999.
[5] Mary Ann Mason and Ann Quirk, "Are Mothers Losing Custody? Read My Lips: Trends in Judicial Decision-Making in Custody Disputes—1920, 1960, 1990 and 1995," ***Family Law Quarterly 31*** **(Summer 1997); 231.**

effective custody evaluator, a psychologist should have a degree at the doctoral level in psychology; several years of hands-on postdoctoral experience; a solid base of experience and knowledge relating to child, adolescent, and adult development; and a full understanding of family dynamics, including the effects of divorce.[4]

4. Psychiatrist. A psychiatrist is a medical doctor. Psychiatrists, while lagging far behind psychologists in use, are nonetheless the second most commonly used expert in custody litigation.[5] Unfortunately, psychiatrists are not very well trained to do intensive patient evaluations or extensive talk therapy. Psychiatrists focus primarily on diagnosis of mental illness and prescription and regulation of medication. Obviously, a psychiatrist is not normally your expert of choice in a custody battle. Aside from being notoriously expensive, they frequently are unavailable to testify at trial. Consequently, as with other doctors, you may have to submit deposition testimony to the court. Clearly, a dry transcript is not as persuasive as a good witness testifying in person. In summary, I try to avoid using psychiatrists in custody cases unless there is some pressing pharmacological or neurological issue.

The Professional Evaluation

At some point before trial, you are likely to be sent to a professional, perhaps a psychologist, whose job it is to do an evaluation of you. This process may come by way of an order from the court that is typically addressed to both parties, as well as to the children. Although the court can initiate this process on its own motion, the motion of one of the parties typically triggers it. In some

[6] Mary Ann Mason and Ann Quirk, "Are Mothers Losing Custody? Read My Lips: Trends in Judicial Decision-Making in Custody Disputes—1920, 1960, 1990 and 1995," ***Family Law Quarterly 31*** **(Summer 1997); 232.**

jurisdictions, because of constitutional concerns, courts are reluctant to order the parties to submit themselves to such an evaluation absent a showing of good cause. Studies suggest that experts are approved by the court in approximately 50 percent of cases.

Alternatively, in cases in which the court does not issue such an order to the parties, each party is free to find his own expert for trial. This approach does have the shortcoming previously discussed, namely that such an expert is restricted in terms of what conclusions or opinions he can state. However, despite an inability to opine as to the identity of the preferred primary custodial parent, the retained expert can nonetheless say a great deal. He can comment on Dad's mental health, his personality, and his positive parenting attributes. He can comment on whether an accused alcoholic or spousal abuser is in fact those things. Where the evaluator is permitted to evaluate the children as well, he can comment on Dad's relationship with the kids, the kids' personalities and needs, and Dad's ability to meet those needs. Obviously, there are many other subjects an expert can address, but he must stop short of the following comparative conclusion: "In my opinion Dad would be the best primary custodial parent."

The evaluation itself consists of stages. The first stage might be termed the "setup." This is the point at which the evaluator first becomes acquainted with the case. Most evaluators prefer to communicate initially with a client representative or one of the attorneys to determine the following:

- the basic facts of the case;
- who the client or clients will be (whether one or both parents will participate and whether the children will be evaluated);
- the scope of the evaluation (Is the evaluator to focus upon specific allegations, such as domestic violence or alcoholism, or is the evaluation more in the nature of a comprehensive inquiry as to which should be the primary custodial parent?); and
- the not insignificant question of who is to pay.

If both parties participate, payment is normally allocated on ratios of income. In either case, money must be deposited with the evaluator, unless of course the evaluator is paid from some other source, such as the court system. The setup may also include an initial meeting with the client or clients for the purpose of getting the necessary documents signed. These documents include a retainer agreement (contract for services), payment of retainer, "informed consent" statement, waiver of confidentiality (giving evaluator the right to disclose findings to court and opposing counsel), and various medical, educational, and other releases.

The next phase involves information gathering and an analysis of the results. During this stage, the evaluator meets with the client or clients on a substantive level and often will talk further with his counsel or both counsels if both parties are to be included.

On the basis of these interviews and the scope of the evaluation, the evaluator then develops a plan for determining his conclusions. In developing the plan, the psychologist will determine which interviews would be helpful, which will, of course, vary on the basis of the objective and the individual case. If there is a custody dispute, a conscientious psychologist will typically talk to the children's day care providers, teachers, extended family members, prior counselors, treating physicians, and, if applicable, new spouses or significant others. Again, the information sought will vary with the objective. Commonly, however, the psychologist will inquire as to the children's behavior, their health status, and their attitudes.

The interviewer will ask about each parent's interaction with the interviewee and the interviewee's familiarity with each parent. The interviewer may investigate alleged incidents during these interviews. A psychologist will commonly invest 20 to 25 hours in interviews. These interviews will likely include all knowledgeable figures in the children's lives, including teachers, day care providers, health care professionals, and therapists. Psychologists term the information gleaned from this method "subjective data," but such sources are immensely useful in giving a fuller and more accurate picture. The evaluator must be able to obtain third-party perspectives to test the validity of what he hears from the parties, as well as to gain insight and knowledge that the parties do not possess.

In addition to interviews, a psychologist will administer certain tests to the client or clients and the children. The appropriate tests are, of course, determined by the objective. In a custody battle, the psychologist will typically give a battery of tests. The tests are either objective (e.g., multiple choice), in which where the individual has no room for discretion beyond stated choices, or projective, in which the individual is allowed latitude in the response and behavior and other factors are also considered. As a result, a projective test is more difficult to score. An example of a projective test is one in which the individual is asked to draw pictures.

This aspect of the evaluation process is discussed more fully below. It is not uncommon, however, for testing of a parent and the children to require a total of three to five hours.

In addition to interviews and testing, it is helpful to give the evaluator any other sources of information that might make his conclusions more credible at trial. Examples include journals kept by either party and letters and notes written by either party. Another important source that many lawyers neglect is the discovery materials obtained during the pendency of the case (interrogatories, requests for admissions, and deposition transcripts). The expert's authority is greatly enhanced by having considered this additional information, particularly when he did not have a chance to hear it directly from Mom.

After the information-gathering stage comes the analysis and conclusions phase. This is the point at which the evaluator views the data before him and arrives at his "opinions." Often there is a report prepared at this point, which states these opinions and their basis.

The report is commonly 15 to 25 pages in length. The report will disclose all sources of information used (e.g., interviews, tests, and discovery materials, such as depositions, and original documents, such as letters or journals).

The report will likely provide a brief statement of the problem or task. It will recount briefly the history of the relationship and data on items like the length of marriage and ages of children. Each subject evaluated, whether parent or child, should be discussed individually, as well as his or her relationship with the other subjects.

A well-written report will also contain references to the custody criteria of the governing statute in detailing the basis for any custodial opinion.[7]

Sometimes a strategic decision is made that a report either will not be prepared or will be prepared closer to trial. The reason is simple: the more information your opponent has regarding your position and the sooner she has it, the better she is able to counter it. For example, I certainly prefer that my expert have a copy of the report by my opponent's expert before writing his. Once you have named someone as your expert, however, which you will probably be forced to do either in answer to an interrogatory or deposition question or because of a procedural rule, that person is subject to deposition, and any report he has can be obtained by opposing counsel.

Note, however, that your lawyer may retain an expert preliminarily to do an evaluation primarily for purposes of determining whether the person would be helpful as an expert. Your lawyer will carefully refrain from naming him as an expert. During that phase, the expert's information and opinions are not reachable by the other side because it is considered "attorney work-product," which means it is privileged and non-discoverable. Once, of course, you decide to use the person and name him as an expert, he is susceptible to inquiry, as previously discussed.

[7] **Betty Clark, "Acting in the Best Interest of the Child: essential Components of a Child Custody Evaluation,"** ***Family Law Quarterly 29*** **(Spring 1995): 35-36.**

In 1996, a survey was conducted of 800 psychologists who performed child custody evaluations. The psychologists were asked to estimate the amount of time they spent on various aspects of an evaluation. The results are as follows: [8]

Activity	Mean hours spent in activity
Observations	2.6
Reviewing materials	2.6
Collateral contacts	1.6
Psychological testing	5.2
Report writing	5.3
Interviewing parents	4.7
Interviewing children	2.7
Interviewing significant others	1.6
Consulting with attorneys	1.2
Testifying in court	2.2

Regarding costs of psychological experts, the Ackerman study showed an average hourly fee of $120.63 for conducting the evaluation and an hourly rate of $154.77 for testifying at trial. The fees for evaluations ranged from $650 to $15,000.[9] The average cost was $2,645.96. This is consistent with recent experience.

The first test most commonly used in custody disputes is the Minnesota Multiphasic Personality Inventory (MMPI).

A second common test is the MMPI 2 and MMPIA. This test has been around since 1937 and is the most frequently used test in custody evaluations. It consists of approximately 567 multiple-choice questions. This test is intended to identify psychological problems. As a layperson, it is virtually impossible to identify what each question

[8] Marc J. Ackerman and Melissa C. Ackerman, "Child Custody Evaluation Practices: A 1996 Survey of Psychologists," *Family Law Quarterly 30* (Fall 1996): 569.
[9] Marc J. Ackerman and Melissa C. Ackerman, "Child Custody Evaluation Practices: A 1996 Survey of Psychologists," *Family Law Quarterly 30* (Fall 1996): 575.

is targeting. In fact, numerous questions are there simply to see if you are trying to steer the test results a particular way. This test is perhaps the most reliable and influential single test available to measure these various personality characteristics. Its reliability is enhanced by the fact that it has as a sample thousands of subjects in very different settings, for instance, schools, places of employment, and prisons, over a 50-year period. In 1989, the test was modified somewhat to make it more current. The new version is MMPI 2. Also in 1991, a version was created specifically for adolescents, the MMPIA. Its questions target areas more relevant to teens, for instance, peer pressure, parental authority, and school.

The test is difficult to manipulate. If you attempt to be perfect, admit no faults, and betray no fears, your K and L scales will show suspiciously high levels, thereby casting doubt on the reliability of the test. I should add that some defensiveness is normal; after all, the test taker realizes that it is important to not be perceived as having psychosis or schizophrenia. Psychologists say that the test taker should answer "optimistically truthfully." This means that only on doubtful calls do you choose the more positive or optimistic alternative. Never consciously choose a response you know is untrue. The test is smarter than you.

Another popular test administered in custody disputes is the Millon Clinical Multaxial Inventory (MCMI) II and III. MCMI-II and MCMI-III tests were originally published in 1983. The first revised version (MCMI-II) came out in 1987, and a newer version has since been released (MCMI-III). The test is a pencil and paper test with 175 items. Unlike the MMPI, which used as its testing data a normal population (i.e., people outside clinical care settings), the MCMI is based on a clinical population of people who were either inpatients or outpatients receiving mental health care around the country. As a result, this test is not recommended for normal subjects. Because of the sampling pool, a normal subject is likely to show greater problems than he in fact has; that is, there is a high rate of "false positive" results. Despite this fact, surveys show a substantial increase in its use by psychologists in custody evaluations.[10]

The MCMI tests for 22 personality disorders. It also has several scales (areas of measurement based on various clusters of questions) intended to detect when a subject is not being truthful (called validity scales). Although these indicators are likely not as reliable as those for the MMPI, it nonetheless behooves you to answer them candidly. Like the MMPI, a readiness to concede shortcomings may actually enhance your overall performance. Remember that the evaluator is looking for good, and not perfect, parents. Therefore, if you show defensiveness, this will only raise concerns and questions in the evaluator's mind.

I will simply note here that the MCMI is not intended for subjects under age the age of 18. For this group, there is the Millon Adolescent Personality Inventory, which consists of 150 true-false items (called MAPI).

The Personality Inventory for Children is a pen and paper test with 420 true-false items. One of the parents takes the test. The purpose of the test is to determine the child's status emotionally, socially, and intellectually.

The theory underlying the test is that objective conclusions can be reached about how well a child is doing by asking specific reasonably objective questions of the parent. An involved parent will possess the source information, for instance, school performance, peer relationships, and disobedience, with which broad but reliable conclusions can be reached about how well the child is presently doing. As you might suspect, one parent or the other may have an incentive to distort the answers to this test. If Mom has been the primary nurturer and represents the status quo, then she has an incentive to manufacture a favorable assessment. Similarly, Dad may

[10] Marc J. Ackerman and Melissa C. Ackerman, "Child Custody Evaluation Practices: A 1996 Survey of Psychologists," ***Family Law Quarterly 30*** **(Fall 1996): 573.**

have the opposite incentive for the same reason. Therefore, the test has three scales built into it, which are intended to illuminate this problem. One of these, the "Lie Scale" is designed to detect exaggeratedly positive responses wherein a child is portrayed as having virtually no flaws or difficulties.

The above objective tests require the test taker to give one of three responses: yes, no, or "I don't know." The test is scored by simply tabulating the responses to some portion or the entire test. As you would expect, computers usually score these tests. Projective tests, on the other hand, allow the subject more freedom of expression. Not only is the substantive answer significant, but also significant is the way it is expressed (tone, gestures, inflection, and demeanor). Obviously scoring such tests leaves more room for interpretation, but this disadvantage is thought to be outweighed by the reduced probability of dissimulation and the broader array of factors considered. There are three projective tests that are commonly used in custody disputes.

Perhaps the best known is the Rorschach psychodiagnostic test. This test is more commonly known as the "Rorschach inkblot test." Hermann Rorschach, who died in 1922, originally developed the test in 1911. Since then, various psychologists have developed several systems for interpreting the responses. The test itself comprises ten 7 x 9-inch cards. Each card has an inkblot. Five cards are gray and black, two cards have red added to the gray and black, and three cards are in pastel colors.

The exact manner in which the test is given varies according to the system being used. The psychologist may face you or sit beside you. The point is for you to focus on the cards and not the test giver or his notes. The test giver will say as few words to you as possible, with the concern being that during the test he not say anything to contaminate the results. After some brief and vague instructions, the test giver will normally hand you one card at a time going from cards I through X and saying with each, "What might this be?" The test generally lasts 45 minutes to one hour. The purpose of the whole exercise is for you to say what you see on each card.

The examiner will write your answers down verbatim. He will also record your nonverbal responses (facial gestures and movements). After going through all 10 cards, the examiner will then do an "inquiry"; that is, in a brief and nonleading way, he will go over each answer, reading it back to the subject and inquiring as to the reason it appeared as the subject said it did. The examiner should make the inquiry as brief and to-the-point as possible.

In scoring the test, the examiner will look at five aspects of the test:

1) the portion of each picture you focused on (the location)
2) the characteristic of each picture that triggered the answer (color and shape; the "determinants")
3) the actual content of the answer given (animal, plant, clothing, and human anatomy; the "content")
4) the answers very commonly given. Not surprisingly, many people give the same response ("popular responses")
5) the total number of responses. It is common for each test taker to give a total of 30 to 40 responses to the ten pictures.

The interpretation of the responses is far too complex to be covered here in any detail. Keep in mind that the interpretation is to consider the Rorschach responses in conjunction with the subject's other test scores, as well as information about the subject obtained from interviews and other empirical sources.

Having said this, a few comments are helpful regarding each area of scoring. Regarding location, responses are categorized as referring to the whole picture, major details, and minor details of the empty space. A healthy range of answers in which major details were the basis is 30 percent to 75 percent. Fewer than 30 percent suggests an unwholesome lack of interest in details, and over 75 percent suggests obsession with detail.

Regarding determinants, there are four dimensions: color, form, movement, and shading. The most common categories of answers are anatomy, animal, and human. A normal response will be based 30 percent to 50 percent on form. A greater than 50 percent response based on form is unfavorable in that it suggests stereotypical thinking. Conversely, a less than 30 percent response based on form suggests that the subject is directed too much by emotion.

Regarding movement, a normal score will have two through four responses based on the perception of human activity (people running or man fishing).

Regarding shading (use of the gray areas of each blot), a normal response would not include more than one of these. Additional use may indicate depression or anxiety.

Content is complex. Generally, it is favorable for responses to come from a variety of categories as opposed to coming predominantly from a few. The latter suggests some sort of unreality preoccupation or obsession. Of particular significance in custody disputes is the number of responses relating to humans, including humans engaged in normal human activities.

Regarding popular responses, one system identifies 21 popular responses. It is normal to have seven to nine of these. More than ten is generally unfavorable because it suggests overconforming or worse evasiveness or defensiveness. Fewer than seven popular responses may indicate an unhealthy iconoclasm.

Regarding the total number of responses, greater is generally more favorable than fewer. This, however, assumes that the content is appropriate. Again, a low number of responses may indicate evasiveness, defensiveness, or lack of intelligence.

In addition to the aforementioned "personality tests," there are a number of tests designed specifically for use in child custody disputes. Although the former test relates only indirectly to the issues of parental fitness and parent-child relationships, these latter tests target custody issues head-on.

Before discussing each of these tests, it is helpful to group the underlying values that psychologists use to determine suitability and preference. Perhaps most important, according to two leading psychologists in the field, are the following factors:

- A positive attitude toward the other parent. Willingness to minimize disruption to the child's life and activities (school, friends, or relatives).
- Level of parenting skills (empathy, communication, discipline, understanding of the child, and ability to teach).
- Consistency with reasonable flexibility.
- A healthy attachment to the child (as opposed to dependency).[11]

Other traits generally regarded by psychologists as important to primary parenting include each parent's relationships with their parents, willingness to give affection, role modeling, desire to teach and demonstrate good character traits, and appreciation for good health habits.[12] With these factors in mind, the following tests are the most commonly used to directly evaluate child custody concerns.

The Ackerman-Schoerdorp Scale for Parent Evaluation of Custody (ASPECT), according to its author, is the most frequently used custody test for adults.[13] This test is purely a creature of the professional literature regarding parental fitness. In creating the test, the originators perused the most authoritative psychological studies and

[11] Chasin and Grovenebaum, "A Model for Evaluation in Custody Disputes," American Journal of Family Therapy 9 (1981): 43-47.

[12] Barnard and Jensen, "Child Custody Evaluation: A Rational Process for an Emotion-Laden Event," *American Journal of Family Therapy 13* (1984): 61-67.

[13] Marc J. Ackerman and Melissa C. Ackerman, "Child Custody Evaluation Practices: A 1996 Survey of Psychologists," *Family Law Quarterly 30* (Fall 1996): 574.

identified 56 characteristics important to a custody determination. These variables are examined by way of three subscales: observational, social, and emotional/cognitive. Put differently, one scale is based on the parent's appearance and demeanor as observed by the examiner (called self-presentation). The other is based on the parent's relationships with others (the child, the extended family, the other spouse, and the community). The final category is based on the parent's psychological health (mental and emotional well-being).

The ASPECT is in some ways an eclectic test. Its originators looked at each variable mentioned and carefully considered what source would provide the most reliable information as to that characteristic. As one would expect, information on certain characteristics could be gleaned by simply meeting and interacting with the person and asking the parent appropriate questions, whereas others might be best determined by investigating factors such as educational history, medical records, history of alcohol abuse, and organizational involvement. Finally, some variables may only be reliably assessed by objective and projective testing, such as the MMPI and Rorschach tests.

The originators appear to have set out to design the perfect custody examination, incorporating the best of the most important examinations currently in use. As a parent-subject, there is a limited range of opportunities to favorably affect the outcome of the test. Among the things you cannot affect is the empirical history (academic, medical, and social history). That record will speak for itself.

You cannot positively affect the tests your child may take. There is some question as to whether you can dramatically affect your own test scores in a favorable manner. You can control your appearance, your attitude, and your demeanor. You can be pleasant and punctual in the interview. You can prepare for a written examination called the "parent questionnaire," which asks you details about your child's life (his school, his health, and his day-to-day care), by knowing names, times, and details. You can choose to speak positively in the interview of the opposing party. Finally, subject to the limitations previously mentioned, you can do your best on the other testing by following the instructions in this book.

In scoring the test, the examiner will answer either "up," "down," or "don't know" to each of the 56 variables using the prescribed source for each. If both parents are participating, which is obviously the preferred approach, each parent is scored. If no significant difference results, the test does not suggest that either is a better primary custodial parent. A significant difference is normally equivalent to one standard deviation, which is defined as a 10-point difference in the "T-score," with the mean T-score being 50, although the 10-point rule is not without exception. Some of the 56 items are obviously more important than others. If the difference is accounted for by the least important items, then 10 points may not be significant. Conversely, if an overwhelming fact exists, such as severe and persistent alcoholism or pedophilia, this may only affect a few of the 56 factors and therefore not significantly impair that parent's T-score. Nonetheless, it is safe to assume that despite the ASPECT score, that parent will not see primary custody soon.

The Bricklin Perceptual Scales (BPS) test was developed by Barry Bricklin, PhD, in the early 1960s. Until its publication in 1984, it was used primarily in research relating to custody matters. Since 1984, the test has gained popularity in part because of its validity, as measured by its correspondence with judges' ultimate decisions in custody litigation, as well as its high correlation with other reputable tests, for instance, ASPECT. The results also show consistency over time. It is the most frequently used custody test for children.[14]

The test is based on a simple foundational belief that children themselves are the best source of information as to the effectiveness of each parent's parenting. The test is not so boorish, however, as to directly ask the kids who is a better parent.

[14] Marc J. Ackerman and Melissa C. Ackerman, "Child Custody Evaluation Practices: A 1996 Survey of Psychologists," ***Family Law Quarterly 30*** **(Fall 1996): 574.**

TACTICAL INFORMATION

The Bricklin Perceptual Scales (BPS) is the most frequently used custody test for children.

14

Instead, Bricklin identified 32 variables that were commonly regarded as important to good parenting and then created a set of questions to be answered by the child with regard to each parent (a total of 64 questions). However, the questions do not call for a simple up or down vote. Instead, the child is given a chance to respond verbally and also nonverbally on each question. The child is shown a card for each question. The card shows a scale. On one side is "very well," and on the other is "not so well," with a 7.5-inch black line between them. The child is given a stylus and asked to punch a point along the line where the parent falls with regard to each question. What the child does not see is the back of the card, which shows points along the line numbering 1 to 60.

As you have probably already figured out, the parent of choice is the one with the highest total score. A parent's score can range from 0 to 1920 points (32 x 60). The originators suggest that a difference of 40 or more points on any given card between parents indicates an important issue to the child and should be examined further. Also, a difference in total scores of more than 300 points is unusual and should be investigated further. The difference could be due to what Bricklin calls "mind mode up". This indicates cases in which the child may have been programmed or otherwise improperly influenced. Usually, the child's answers are summary, not credibly defended, and prompt. Eye contact is poor, and the child will avoid friendly discussion.

When you send your child in for such a test, you must count on the seeds you have sown over the years to yield fruit. The test is not gender biased. If your child answers honestly, this should accrue to your benefit; if not, you need to reappraise this entire project. It is definitely clear that coaching will likely fail, and you will be penalized for your attempt in the psychologist's report and, I suspect, in the judge's decision.

The perception of relationships test (PORT) is another test developed by Dr. Barry Bricklin. It was first published in 1990, although it was originally developed in the 1970s.

The PORT is a measure of how much the child seeks and/or experiences emotional closeness with each parent. There are seven tasks, mostly involving drawing. The parent favored on the majority of the seven tasks is referred to as the "parent of choice." According to the PORT, this means that the child is more strongly emotionally attached or bonded to the parent of choice. As you might imagine, relative strength of emotional attachment to each parent is a critical factor in most child custody cases. The parent to whom the child is more strongly bonded is sometimes referred to as the "primary attachment figure." The PORT was validated in much the same fashion as the BPS (against judge's rulings and the ratings of mental health professionals familiar with cases in which children completed the PORT). Like the BPS, the PORT is widely used in custody evaluations. Also like the BPS, its strength is in giving a "child's eye view" of each parent. When used as part of a comprehensive child custody evaluation, including other psychological testing and interviews, the BPS and PORT can be powerful ways to show a child's feelings and preferences without putting the child in the potentially difficult position of having to state their opinions openly.

9

Trial Preparation: Tools, Tactics and Techniques

I never see one of Jackson's couriers
approach without expecting an
order to assault the North Pole.

-CSA Maj. Gen. Richard Ewell

Introduction

In a custody dispute, one of the greatest challenges in preparing for trial is to gather evidence in a form usable in court. Invariably both parties have very different claims. The parties will disagree about the historical facts of their parenting and their marriage. Mom often exaggerates her role in various nurturing activities. She will often overstate Dad's work schedule or recreational interests. She may elevate Dad's occasional alcohol consumption to the level of abuse. Conversely, Mom rarely concedes any ground regarding Dad's complaints about her.

Regarding future circumstances (work schedules, health issues, and relocation plans), the parties' testimony is likely to be widely divergent. Similarly, regarding those stated issues previously discussed (Dad's qualities and attributes versus those of Mom), further conflict can be expected.

Therefore, you might wonder whether a trial is simply an exercise in "he said-she said" exchanges. Without preparation, it would be, and as to some issues, it still is, irrespective of the amount of preparation. Fortunately, over the centuries methods have evolved as part of the litigation process that are calculated to allow truth to distill to the surface. In this chapter I will discuss the nuts and bolts of when and how to use these and other sources to your advantage, both offensively and defensively.

Contrary to the popular model of trial, which naively calls for each lawyer to deliver to the court all the relevant information useful to its decision, the reality is that each lawyer will deliver only that information that helps his or her case. Paradoxically, however, that is enough according to orthodox litigation theology. This model simply asserts that the adversarial process will bring the truth to light. This is more an expression of faith than fact. In practice, one side may prevail over the other, even though the facts are not on his or her side. Unfortunately, cases are determined more by skillful lawyers, financial resources, and blind luck. One such example has become a poster child for this point: the case of O. J. Simpson. There is, however, an important distinction between your case and his: he had a largely uneducated and unintelligent group of laypersons as his fact finders. Conversely, you will likely have a battle-hardened and intelligent professional. Nonetheless, the judge can be, and often is, influenced by nonfact elements.

TACTICAL INFORMATION 15

Your attorney's ethical duty, within the framework of honesty and fair play, is to see to it that you win.

Simply put, your attorney's ethical duty, within the framework of honesty and fair play as embodied in the rules of professional ethics, is to see to it that you win. He owes no duty to your wife and in fact owes no duty to your children. His job is to help you get what you want.

That said, let us discuss how this general objective, this war aim, is to be implemented on the ground.

As discussed previously in the introductory chapter, your attorney's task is to assemble and put before the court all evidence that will favorably impress the judge and minimize the presentation of any evidence likely to adversely influence the judge. Again, this war must be waged according to certain rules of engagement that relate to honesty and fairness. Despite what you may have heard about the legal profession, I can tell you that no reputable (or even rational) lawyer would jeopardize his license to practice law for any client. Do not expect your lawyer to lie to the other lawyer, lie to the court, or, where he has knowledge, permit you to lie. Furthermore, your lawyer will not participate in any frauds on the court, for instance, misrepresentations regarding income and assets. If you do retain a lawyer that is so inclined, dump him. If others cannot trust him, neither can you.

TACTICAL INFORMATION 16

If you retained a lawyer that is inclined to put forward misrepresentations, dump him. If others cannot trust him, neither can you!

Subject, however, to these modest constraints, your lawyer should aggressively pursue your goals. One of the primary ways he does this is to prepare for trial.

Assembling a Witness List

Your input is essential here. You are painting a picture for the court. You need additional voices to make that picture as vivid and credible as possible. Witnesses fall into one of two categories: lay and expert. A lay witness may be a professional. These witnesses are sometimes called "fact" witnesses. In other words, they are not created for trial. I often will ask my client for names of people who have been around the parties and the kids a lot, most importantly in the home. The witnesses need to be credible, articulate, neat, and sincere.

School employees, such as teachers and counselors, are often credible witnesses. They can often discuss the level of participation and interest of each parent. They may also have observed the kids interacting with the parents. Also, depending on possible evidentiary constraints, they may be able to discuss statements made to them by the kids. Academic performance may also be at issue.

Frequently useful are health care providers, both those of the parents and the kids, depending on what is being alleged. It should be noted, however, that as to a parent, federal and state laws severely restrict access to medical records. Typically, "good cause" must be shown, although abuse or neglect of children is usually sufficient.

Divorced Dad's Tip:

When preparing your case, your attorney will assemble a list of witnesses who can attest to your relationship with your children – teachers, coaches, Boy Scout leaders, grandparents and other relatives. In building your case, these people will be able to attest to your ongoing and dedicated relationship with your children. You are fighting for your right to continue being involved in your children's lives. Because that's what you've been doing since they were born. It is very difficult for a judge to ignore the testimony of a dozen witnesses who say you've never missed a ballgame or a flute practice since they've known you.

Clients often ask how many witnesses they should have. The answer depends, in part, on how many good witnesses are available and in part on the time constraints imposed by the court. Obviously if you do not have to ration time, you would put on all available helpful witnesses, both expert and lay witnesses. In busier courts (often in urban areas), judges will prescribe a fixed amount of time with which you must present your entire case. Obviously, the time allotted will vary with the number and complexity of issues. If only custody is in dispute, judges in St. Louis County will often assign your case one day for trial, which means three to four hours for each party. I should add that apart from express time limitations, there is an implicit expectation on the part of all courts that you not waste the court's time with cumulative or marginally relevant evidence.

Subject, however, to these conditions, it is often better to err on the side of too many witnesses rather than too few. An attorney will often have more witnesses present than will be called to testify. When in doubt, a capable attorney will subpoena or otherwise ensure the presence of a witness and then decide whether he is needed as the trial unfolds.

The Role of Private Investigators

Many people have an image of ugly divorces in which private detectives are sitting outside motel rooms. Although this image sometimes mirrors real life, it does not in most cases. Usually, private detectives are used to document marital misconduct, e.g., infidelity, dissipation of assets, and fraud, and are not used as regularly in custody disputes. As has been discussed, misconduct is often not relevant to the issue of custody. To be relevant to custody, the conduct must relate tangibly to the quality of one's parenting.

Divorce lawyers often use private investigators to document a parent's substance abuse. If alcoholism is alleged, it is helpful to observe the amount of alcohol consumed and then to note whether that parent then drives a vehicle. This is not as difficult as it sounds. If Mom goes to a bar or another public place, the private investigator simply goes in and observes. He can thereafter follow the vehicle and testify not only to the quantity of alcohol consumed but also to the manner in which the vehicle is driven. He may contact law enforcement officials if the alcohol consumption is substantial.

If it is alleged that Mom is not in fact caring for children when in her custody, a private investigator can document the evenings she goes out and where the children are left.

If Mom claims she cannot work because of physical limitations, videotape can quickly dispose of that allegation.

If Mom has a boyfriend, this may be relevant to custody if he consumes much of her time or if he is a bad guy. If Mom concedes that her relationship with the boyfriend is serious, (believe it or not, this is commonly admitted, proving that love is not just blind but dumb as well), this puts the boyfriend at issue. Is he divorced? What allegations did his wife make in their divorce? Would she testify to those things now? You might also have his police record checked.

In considering the use of a private investigator, you must be able to prescribe, as narrowly as possible, the time frames in which the private investigator is to be on the job. Remember that his meter is running at an hourly rate of $40 to $60. Therefore, you need to identify windows of time during which the conduct you suspect will occur. Some things the private investigator can do for you on a project basis, which is a fixed fee. These include checking driving records, police records, or locating addresses.

Interrogatories

These are simply typed questions sent to the other side that must be answered and returned within a given period of time (usually 30 days). The answers are sworn to be truthful and carry a perjury penalty, just as does live testimony in court. These are sometimes used instead of the more costly alternative, a deposition. Usually, however, interrogatories are used in conjunction with depositions. The interrogatories are set early in the case to obtain information useful in preparing for the deposition.

The receiving party must answer the questions or make a valid objection as to why she will not. If you are on the receiving end, answer the questions carefully. If your lawyer does not initiate it, call your lawyer and set up a time to review your answers with him or someone in his office before the answers are typed up and sent out.

What you say in your interrogatories is under oath, and you are to some extent wedded (pardon the phrase) to it. Therefore, your answers should be true and complete. Ensure that they are.

Depositions

A deposition is simply testimony given before the trial. In a divorce, depositions will typically take place in one of the lawyer's conference rooms. Present will be you, your wife, the two lawyers, a court reporter, and, if the deposition is of someone other than a party, the "deponent" (the one whose deposition is being taken). The deposition itself consists of a lawyer asking questions of the deponent. Typically, the deposition of each party is done on the same day. The total time necessary for both depositions varies widely, depending again on the number and complexity of the issues. The custody issues themselves could require four hours for each party, but for the vast majority of divorces, the depositions of both parties are completed in less than eight hours. If one is not completed on the scheduled date, then it is continued to another date.

The tenor of a deposition can be informal, unstructured, and even friendly. Alternatively, it can be very formal and regimented, with numerous exhibits (documents the deponent is questioned about) and heated cross-examination. Most depositions lie somewhere between these two extremes.

My experience has been that the atmosphere of any given deposition is determined primarily by the questioning attorney's personality and secondarily by his strategy. The fact that some attorneys are jerks, particularly after doing divorce law for ten years, worsens matters because many clients believe that such behavior is the hallmark of a good divorce lawyer. Therefore, although it may serve no rational purpose, some lawyers, as a matter of course, will seek to intimidate or embarrass you or your witnesses at a deposition. Most attorneys, thankfully, do not behave this way. The best lawyers will make a determination going in as to what tone or style best serves their client's needs with that particular witness in that particular case. Do not get me wrong, there are occasions when an aggressive confrontational demeanor at a deposition is the most effective strategy. However, more frequently, in my opinion, a kinder, gentler tone in a deposition produces more yardage. To understand this statement, let me explain more fully the purposes of a deposition.

Purposes of the Deposition

The deposition serves essentially two critical and overlapping purposes in a divorce.

First and foremost, it allows you to "peek behind the curtain," so to speak, to get a preview of what the deponent will say at trial. When the deponent is your wife, the value of this sneak preview cannot be overestimated. If the deposition goes as planned, you are given a wonderful opportunity to hear your wife's trial testimony weeks or months before trial: her accusations, her arguments, and even her specific demands and each event or circumstance (real or contrived) that underlies those positions. Although she can change her testimony at trial, you do not have to be a lawyer to predict that she will pay a heavy price in terms of her credibility with the court if she does so. Her deposition testimony can be used with great dramatic effect at trial to expose a contradicting witness.

Another, and perhaps just as important, advantage of this preview is that it affords you the opportunity to observe your wife (and others as the case may be) testify. By "observe," I refer to all those factors, apart from simple content, that affect someone's credibility. No transcript or other printed word is a substitute for this impression. By observing the other side's demeanor and tone, you can see what the judge will see. Does your wife come across as sincere? Is she articulate? Does she appear fair-minded? Can she be provoked? I have settled cases on the basis of the demeanor of a party after deposition. The fact is that some people testify very badly; they are neither likeable nor believable. Attorneys can help such a client or other witness by carefully prepping them beforehand, but obviously, this damage control has its limitations.

If that is so, there are probably additional sources of evidence to bolster your testimony. Furthermore, I discuss below some rules to help maximize your potential as a witness both in deposition and at trial.

The second important purpose of a deposition is to obtain information, such as the names and addresses of important figures (boyfriends, supervisors, customers, witnesses, and health care providers) and sources of income. It is important to get this information before trial so that you and your lawyer can follow up with further discovery to better build your case. This information may be used offensively or defensively. You are hopefully afforded sufficient time to locate evidence confirming your claims and contradicting hers. As discussed earlier, your case is built primarily of facts. This is a useful means of obtaining them.

Topics You Can Expect

The following is an outline of topics that may be covered both in your deposition and that of your wife.

- Background: name, address, employment, and age.
- Your health. Is your health good? Any problems? Names and addresses of health care providers over the past five years. For what reason and for what kind of treatment did you see a doctor? What is the prognosis (subject to a privilege objection)?
- Spouse's health. Is her health good? If not, explain. If your spouse's health is at issue, you will be asked in detail about her history, as you understand it.
- Your living conditions: house, apartment, or other. Plans to

move? Describe. Floor plan? Sleeping arrangements? Lease? Describe.

- Wife's living conditions (same as above).
- Your employment. Employment history. Duration of each employment. Reason for leaving. Work schedule for each job. Location of present employer. Future plans.
- Her employment (same as above).
- Children. Names and ages. Are you seeking primary custody? Why? Identify each reason.
- Children's education (as to each child). Grade. Teachers, counselors, and principals to date. Academic history; be as specific as possible. Communications with teachers. Attendance at school events.
- Children's health care (for each child). Each doctor or other provider seen to date. Reason for each identified visit. Who scheduled the appointments? Who took the child?
- Children's care (as to each child). Who changed diapers (give ratio)? Who prepared breakfast (give ratio)? Who served breakfast (give ratio)? Who got the child dressed in the morning (give ratio)? Who prepared dinner (give ratio)? Who served dinner (give ratio)? Who prepared the child for bed (give ratio)? Who gave baths (give ratio)? Who took the child to day care/school (give ratio)? Who picked up the child from day care/school (give ratio)? Who helped with homework (give ratio)? Who spent more time with the child (give ratio)? Who disciplined the child and how (give ratio)?
- Children's activities (as to each child). Identify extracurricular activities. As to each, did you coach? Did your wife? How many events? How many did you attend? How many did your wife attend? Decision-making. Do you and your wife agree regarding issues affecting the children's health, education, and welfare? Do you feel you are capable

of agreeing on such matters in the future? If not, why?
- Financial matters. Expect detailed questions about any income sources.
- Allegations by you (cite each specific incident). Abuse? Neglect? Alcohol problems? Drug abuse? Physical abuse of you (cite each specific incident)? Alienation by wife (city each specific incident)?
- Does wife have any good parenting traits? Describe.

It may not be obvious that the above outline can easily turn into a three to four hour deposition. Keep in mind that a good attorney will not allow a deponent, particularly a party, to get away with sweeping buzz phrases or generalizations. For example, if you state that your wife was "violent" on "numerous" occasions, expect to be asked to define the word "violent" specifically. Then expect the attorney to ask you to identify and describe each and every occasion on which such an event occurred.

Also, it is your attorney's chance to get information you need to pursue other information before trial. In taking a deposition of your wife, your attorney must exercise caution in selecting the topics he will raise. Remember, one of your primary reasons for doing a deposition is to obtain information and not to disburse it. Clients eager to confront their spouses with the damning evidence of their misdeeds are sometimes disappointed when I do not raise particular topics in deposition. However, in taking a deposition you must take the following view: the attorney must weigh the benefit of inquiring about a matter your wife does not expect to be raised at trial (and therefore would otherwise be unprepared for) against the loss of the element of surprise. For example, if you can establish that an incriminating fact exists without any admission from your wife, and if you do not expect an effective denial, you may choose to present such evidence for the first time at trial. Even better, your attorney may ask a broad question that encompasses the incriminating acts and let her take the seductive path of a sweeping denial. Then you adroitly drop the matter until trial. "But what about this thing of 'locking-in' her testimony in the deposition?" you are probably thinking. "If she can't credibly change her testimony at trial, who cares?" It is true that in some sense you lock in her testimony at the deposition, but there are a number of ways, with adequate time and preparation, that the effect can be cushioned, not to mention that the initial fumbling response is not adequately captured on a transcript.

However, in many cases surprise at trial is simply not possible. In this era of liberal and extensive discovery rules, you may be forced to hand over the incriminating information through discovery from the other side. The most likely such occasion is your deposition. As the above outline suggests, the questioning is intended to fill any holes to fully reveal your case. Its objective, in stark contrast to yours, is to prevent surprises.

TACTICAL INFORMATION

17

Do not jeopardize long-term victory for short-term satisfaction by confronting your wife with incriminating evidence on her.

Naturally, when your evidence loses its surprise value, your attorney is free to question your wife about it. Also, regarding surprises, sometimes a tactical decision will be made to disclose unexpected and damaging evidence when you and your attorney believe it will be an impetus to a favorable settlement. I have many times seen such disclosures trigger a quick settlement. In some cases, it was my client that was so triggered.

Therefore, here, as elsewhere in trial preparation, keep your objective in mind. Your goal is to win at trial. As tempting as it is to immediately confront your wife with the salacious and incriminating evidence you may have on her, do not jeopardize long-term victory for short-term satisfaction.

Giving Your Deposition

Let me repeat the primary and overlapping objectives of a deposition of a party: (1) to preview the other side's case and (2) to obtain information.

With these purposes in mind, you can probably guess that your task while being deposed is to provide as little information as possible. This refers not only to raw data, but to the tone, style, and manner of your presentation as well.

During your deposition, you are basically walking a thin line. On the one hand, you have a clear duty to answer the question, unless your attorney instructs you otherwise. The penalty can be harsh if you get to trial and it emerges that you had undisclosed information. Similarly, if you lie, you are subject to criminal prosecution for perjury. That is not good either. On the other hand, absent some overarching settlement strategy (discussed above), you want to communicate only what you must.

In some cases, as the above outline reveals, you will be asked questions regarding which you will need to give knowledgeable answers. For example, you will want to have complete and informed answers to questions concerning the details of the children's education and health care. Paradoxically, this category of questions is intended to reveal your lack of knowledge, and therefore your lack of involvement in nurturing will be argued. For the reasons already discussed, your performance in your deposition is crucial. You should prepare accordingly. Reread this chapter at least a week before your deposition and be prepared to deal with each of the topics raised in the "Topics You Can Expect" section of this chapter. Additionally, irrespective of whether your attorney suggests it, make an appointment to meet with him before the deposition; do not pinch pennies on this one.

Pay particular attention to the following key topics:

- Know by heart the names of all day care providers and/or

teachers past and present. Also, know your child's grades class by class.

- Know from memory all health care providers your children have seen, the reasons for such visits, and any treatment that followed. Know any medications that your children may be taking.
- If you and your wife are proposing different school systems, know comparative data, e.g., class sizes, SAT and PSAT scores, awards, and rankings. Be sure you have visited both schools.
- Expect the following question: why do you believe you should have primary custody? Incidentally, do not unduly demonize Mom; give her credit where credit is due. For reasons discussed in Chapters 7 and 8, it harms your case to swing wildly, to make claims you cannot back up, and to do so in a tone betraying bitterness or anger. You do not want the court to direct its attention from what you say to why you say it, e.g., "of course she loves the kids" versus "of course the kids love her". You do not give up ground in such cases, you just build credibility on the more critical issues.
- In case your lawyer has not told you, go into the deposition with a plan for the future. Be prepared to discuss logistics if you are awarded primary custody, e.g., your work schedule, the time you leave in the morning, when you eat breakfast, location of the day care provider, time of pickup each day, and bus stop location. If you do not have a plan by the time you are in deposition, you need to reconsider the seriousness of your intent.
- If you are alleging misconduct relating to your child, expect to be asked for specifics. Although you should not volunteer them, if pressed, you should be prepared to identify specific instances.

Also, learn and remember the following ground rules regarding all your answers:

- Just answer the question. Provide only enough information to answer the question, but do not volunteer anything. Be succinct. Make the other lawyer work for the information he gets. Once you feel you have answered a question, stop. Silence in the room is okay. It is even good because it means you are not handing over information.
- Do not "make arguments." Remember your opponent's objective. He wants to watch you testify and observe your demeanor, your passion, and your best arguments. You likely will have a lip-biting temptation to give it to him. You will want to give it to him in three-dimensional Technicolor. If you succumb, you have given him the opportunity to give his best rebuttal at trial. No one wins a case in his deposition, but many lose.
- Take a break if you need one. If you become tired or your concentration starts wandering, simply ask for a brief break.
- If you are faced with a crisis, a pivotal question regarding a pivotal issue, and you are completely stumped, you may ask to speak with your counsel. I must tell you that this is frowned on, and the examiner may huff and puff on the record, but it is the lesser of two evils, with the other being that your case self-destructs before your and your lawyer's eyes.
- Do not be intimidated. Clients often have this "bigger than life" view of the other attorney. They think he knows more than he knows, is smarter than he is, and is going to harm them more than he can. If you have prepared properly, and if you are truthful in your answers, you can enter the depositions confidently, knowing you will do your best.
- If you do not know, say so. You have no obligation to know

the answers to all the questions. If you do not know the answer, simply say so, or if you think you are going to have an answer in the future, you might in some cases say, "I don't recall at this time." These are valid responses. In no event should you allow opposing counsel to lure you into speculating or guessing. If opposing counsel persists, politely repeat your answer.

- Do not be led. Your questioner will subtly direct you toward points he wants to establish. It is to some extent human nature to seek to agree. He may in fact assume the demeanor of a friend. The bottom line is that the opposing attorney is your archenemy. When he makes a statement or asks a question that assumes something untrue, interject a correction. Within the bounds of courtesy, make sure your point is made. If you need to interrupt opposing counsel to avoid a misimpression or misstatement, do so.
- Maintain a professional demeanor at all times. The other attorney may attempt to anger you to rattle your cage. He may be rude or sarcastic. However he treats you, do not allow your anger to show. Such repayment in kind reflects badly on you. Leave it to your attorney to intervene when he believes it crosses a line.
- Answer the questions as accurately as you can. Obviously this means being truthful, but beyond that it means not exaggerating your case. Be careful about powerful claims that you cannot back up. This hurts your credibility on the things you can back up.
- Do not bring your records or notes to the deposition unless your attorney specifically tells you to bring them. When you refer to records during a deposition, the other attorney has a right to see them. I extend this rule to include even bringing such documents into the deposition room because it

sometimes triggers lines of questioning and disputes between counsel that could easily have been avoided. Obviously, there are exceptions. In all cases, however, clear it first with your attorney. Feel free to pause and consider your answer. The transcript is the only record, and unless counsel orally notes the pause, the transcript will give no indication of how long you took to answer. Unlike trial, in a deposition taking time for thought is without penalty or prejudice. Feel free to use it.

- If you do not understand a question, say so. You are not punished for asking that the question be rephrased or repeated. In fact, you may misstep seriously if you proceed as if you understand the question when you are really unsure.
- Do not rush to answer. It is important to pause a few seconds after every question to allow your attorney time to insert an objection if he chooses. Additionally, your attorney, like you, could use a second or so to consider his response as well.

Email, Computers and Divorce

Email correspondence is common for both professional and personal purposes. However, there are risks to this type of communication. The primary risk is interception by an unintended recipient. This risk applies to personal emails that you do not want your spouse to see as well as emails from your legal counsel.

Emails can be accessed by anyone who has legitimate access to your computer or your network. Also, anyone who knows your email password can access all of your emails (whether sent or received) once they reach their destination. Password protection of your email accounts or computer files is necessary to keep these communications private.

Another way to prevent interception is to encrypt your emails or computer files. You can do so with computer programs that protect the confidentiality of these communications. Like passwords, these encrypted files can be accessed if someone breaks the encryption. However, this can be complicated for the average person.

Finally, emails can be intercepted by your spouse making a request of the internet service providers (ISPs). These ISPs store emails for varying lengths of time. An ISP can be required to produce the emails in response to a subpoena.

Even if your emails are intercepted, they may not be admissible as evidence in court. Courts will require proof of the authenticity of the email. This means proving who is the author of the email; when was this sent; was it received? Also you must clear the hearsay implications. This means what is the purpose of the email, is it offered to prove the statements it contains, or is it being offered to show that communication occurred at all? In general the best way to have emails admissible as evidence is to request them by subpoena so the ISP can address the authenticity. However, hearsay may still be an issue. Another approach is to have the sender testify about sending the

Divorced Dad's Tip:

Did your mother ever tell you, "If you can't say anything nice, don't say anything at all?" It's good advice in life and divorce. Don't air your dirty laundry in front of your children. It's not healthy for them. It tears them apart. In addition, you should assume that anything you say will work its way back to mom. If your children overhear you saying, "My wife is a dingbat," that comment may eventually work its way to the Judge. The Judge will not be amused that your children are being exposed to demeaning comments about their mother. So always be careful of what you say around the children. This rule should also be applied to letters and emails. These can be produced in court and admitted into evidence. So take a moment to thank your own mother for some really good advice.

email and the receiver testify about receiving it. This approach takes care of the court's evidentiary issues, but as you can imagine this is not always possible. Remember that even if the emails provided are not admissible, they may lead your attorney to other evidence that is.

It is important to know that emails intercepted by an unintended recipient through no fault of the sender or receiver is a crime in some states. This may also be the basis for a civil action against that person depending on the use of the email as well as state law.

As an aside, there are ways to monitor computer activity. A common one is the use of programs that capture key strokes off a keyboard or monitor all Internet activity. Some states have determined that these types of programs are covered by state or federal wire-tapping laws, because they are capturing a transmission of information. Before you even think about using any program like these or intercepting another's email, check with an attorney licensed in your jurisdiction.

Taping

An issue that commonly comes up during a divorce is whether it is okay for one spouse to tape the other, either with video or audio. Naturally, if my client is the one who was taped, he wants to exclude the evidence. If, on the other hand, he has some seriously incriminating stuff that he recorded, he wants to be able to use the tape.

The answer as to when you can tape is a complicated one. There is a federal statute called the Omnibus Crime Control and Safe Streets Act that covers taping and wiretapping. In addition, there are various state statutes governing such taping, although many simply parallel the federal law.

The state and federal statutes impose both criminal and civil liability for violations. Put more directly, you can go to jail and be sued by your wife and others you tape.

Let me first address what you clearly cannot do under both state

TACTICAL INFORMATION

18

The notion of taping is somewhat unsavory to most people, including judges, because of its devious and deceptive nature.

and federal statutes. You cannot record a conversation to which you are not a party. This means you cannot record your wife talking to her boyfriend or others. There used to be a judicially created "spousal exception" to the statutes that permitted such recording until it was abrogated in the 1990s.

Under the federal statute, you may record conversations with one of the participants' consent; the consenting party would, of course, be you. This means you may record conversations you have with your wife and others. Note, however, that this is permitted under the federal statute and in states where state laws mirrors the federal law. Some states may have more restrictive laws. You may recall the furor over whether Linda Tripp could tape Monica Lewinsky without her knowledge. This was not a debate about the federal law, which clearly permitted it. Rather, the alleged illegality related to the Maryland state statute, which did not permit such recording without the consent of both parties. Therefore, confirm that your applicable state statute is consonant with the federal statute before you do any secret taping.

Note that the federal statute and its state counterpart refer to "aural" communications as opposed to soundless video. The federal law and most state statutes permit you to videotape behavior as long as you do not record sound. For example, I recently represented a client who decided to record his wife smoking pot and taking other illicit drugs while the children were in her care. A split screen can be used to vividly make this point, with the wife smoking in the bedroom with the door locked while the kids are playing unattended in the living room. No sound is needed to make the point.

Let me add a cautionary word about taping in general. The notion of taping is somewhat unsavory to most people, judges included. If you doubt this, look no further than the public image of Linda Tripp. By its nature, taping is devious and deceptive. Although it may have significant cachet in the client's mind, it carries a price. Sometimes such a tape tells us as much about the taper as the tapee. The listener finds himself thinking as much about the person whose hand is on the button as about the speaker.

Furthermore, when you tape, you must realize that the tape has no evidentiary value regarding your behavior or conduct during the transaction; obviously you knew the tape was running. In fact, your wife may argue that your demeanor on those recorded occasions contrasts starkly with your less self-conscious expression.

Notwithstanding these disclaimers, tapes can, in some cases, be extraordinarily useful. Nothing condemns like one's own words. However, I would add that a fairly high threshold of usefulness must exist to overcome the pejorative side effects.

For example, I represented a client in a motion for contempt relating to his ex-wife's denial of temporary custody and visitation. He said that he had tapes of her cursing at him and accusing him of not paying support. Might this have been useful? Yes, but not useful enough in my opinion. Suppose, instead, that my client had tapes of Mom expressly refusing visitation for no good reason and with a "to hell with the judge" for good measure. That I would use.

Your Best Behavior

> It is the business of a general
> to be serene and inscrutable,
> impartial and self-controlled.
>
> *-Sun Tzu,*
> *The Art of War,*
> *circa 2000 BC*

From commencement to conclusion, a custody dispute often follows a protracted and sinuous course. In the meantime, the combatants, unfamiliar with this strange new terrain, all too often rely on their instincts and impulses to survive. This is often a disastrous strategy. In a heated divorce, your natural instincts will likely dictate conduct and comments that are directly inconsistent with your objectives. This is understandable given the depth of the offense and the gravity of the dispute. The accompanying welter of feelings provides a poor but powerful compass that unfailingly misdirects your conduct on key occasions.

Let me set the slate. If you are like most men in this situation, you are here because your wife has decided to leave you. In most cases, this desertion is compounded by betrayal when you discover there is another man. The relationship, you discover, has gone on for some time. All this is a desecration of the sacred trust you reserved for no other human being. Then, as if all this were not enough, add the claim she has staked to your children.

In this storm of emotion and events, your words and your deeds are being scrutinized by those who will greatly influence, if not decide, the fate of your children. Your instincts dictate confrontation. Your impulse is to attack at every turn. Your sensibilities have declared a holy war.

Clients in this state of mind always do the wrong things. They fire off caustic and damaging letters to spouses and even their judge. They allow themselves to be drawn into physical and quasi-physical altercations with their wives. They fly off the handle in front of pivotal players (experts, the guardian ad litem, opposing counsel, and even the judge) without inhibition.

Therefore, I think it is critical to lay down some simple ground rules that should guide your every word and deed from start to finish in a custody dispute.

In dealings with your wife, you must always be courteous.

Although this may be counter-intuitive, it is not counter-productive.

As a practical matter, you cannot avoid regular encounters with your wife throughout the process. Each of these occasions presents both a potential problem and an opportunity. Your courtesies to your wife are not intended for her consumption, although a less Machiavellian advisor (a psychologist perhaps) would hurry to point out that such civility is essential to good child-rearing and is therefore a good investment. I do not disagree, but my objective here is more tactical. Your intended recipient of this courtesy on such occasions is not your wife, although only the two of you may be present. As suggested above, there are various important players in this process. It is to them that you direct your performance. Do not dismissively assume that your words to your wife when no one else is present are freebies. I can tell you from years of experience that incriminating communications to your wife will be waved before key players. What is more, these typically streetwise and intelligent people have a remarkable truth-detecting instinct.

Also, I should not neglect another compelling reason for civility in such cases. As discussed before, you may be being taped.

In addition to the purely defensive reasons given above, courteousness is also a powerful weapon. The very forces that expose your missteps on such occasions also illuminate your magnanimity, your forgiving spirit, and your maturity.

Obviously, your courtesies to your wife should extend beyond simple face-to-face encounters. Your most fertile opportunities to score points will be in dealings with third parties, such as schools and health care providers. Obviously, you should weigh your words carefully when speaking to such people regarding your wife. Be sure to instruct such third parties to relay information to your wife.

Related to the courtesy concern is Dad's susceptibility to claims of abuse by Mom. In some cases, dads are heroically challenged to simply avoid being lured into physical and verbal altercations with their spouses. This is to some extent a gender-specific concern. The cry of abuse, it seems, does not ring as persuasively or as alarmingly when emanating from the husband. With that in mind, you must act preemptively and preventively to ensure that your wife is not handed such an opportunity. It is not enough for you to, in fact, avoid such incidents. You must avoid even the prospect of a credible claim.

Another important ground rule relates to how you talk to key figures in the case about your wife. This may be the single biggest mistake most divorcing parents make in custody disputes. I discussed above the natural untutored tendencies of Dad in such circumstances.

In fact, it is because of this tendency that key players, normally the guardian ad litem, psychologists, and/or social workers, will be paying careful attention to your words, acts, and demeanor throughout the divorce. These key players will typically be looking carefully at two concerns: 1. What is your true motivation for pursuing custody? There is often a concern that an angry spouse is lashing out in the way he assumes will hurt the most. 2. What is the probability that you will retaliate against Mom by alienating the children? A parent's perceived propensity to alienate a child from the other parent is a powerful factor in custody disputes.

Therefore, with the above concerns in mind, you can probably distinguish a good answer from a bad one.

Here are some guidelines to follow in your dealings with a key player:[1]

1. Never display hostile feelings toward your wife. Naturally, you are expected to feel displeasure, perhaps even resentment, but keep such emotions under careful check. Do not display wholly negative feelings, such as anger, bitterness, or sarcasm.

2. Unless your wife's adultery ties in tangibly with a custody issue, do not raise the matter, particularly when discussing the subject of custody.
3. Find some good things to say about your wife. Resist the temptation to paint her entirely black. Such concessions greatly enhance your credibility.
4. Readily admit your mistakes and defects when the evidence is there. You should not place your credibility on a sinking ship.
5. Be the first to disclose any damaging facts you know that the other side will raise. If politics has taught us anything, it is the importance of spin control.
6. Know the important historical information regarding your children's health, education, and so on. Such information should include the following: (1) doctors and major illnesses, (2) schools, teachers, and grades, and (3) extracurricular activities.
7. Be prepared to discuss specifically the custodial plan you propose. The more premeditation you display here the better.
8. Be prepared to explain why you believe the plan you propose is best. In doing this, focus on your strengths as opposed to your wife's weaknesses. If, of course, she has a major defect, say, alcoholism or mental illness, you must and should give the matter its deserved attention.
9. Show initiative in your communications. Always be the first parent to contact the key player once he is identified. In such matters, the first word is often better than the last,

[1] The following assumes that the key player is not aligned against you going in, but this is not always the case. Therefore, your attorney should be given the opportunity to review these points before their implementation.

TACTICAL INFORMATION 19

Rely on your attorney to know his turf, the players involved, their relationships and the best combination to arrange for your case.

although you should aspire to both. Furthermore, do not passively wait for the key player to contact you. If you know that a meeting is to occur, initiate the contact. If your attorney says it is okay, you might even keep the key player updated on important developments.

10. Be mindful of your appearance. I wince slightly as I write this section because I realize that for many of you, this point will seem condescending and unnecessary. However, my experience tells me that many men need to hear it. If you are not one of them, skip to the next point. Generally speaking, if your dress is a suit, then wear one on this occasion. If not, wear pressed slacks (no jeans), an ironed button-up shirt, and a tie. Some attorneys will disagree with the necessity of a tie. My reasoning is that it suggests slightly more respect for the key player, as well as a greater concern for the outcome. (This is particularly true if the key player is aware that you added this just for him.) In addition, you should be clean and well groomed. This includes clean nails and combed hair. Again, this communicates respect and concern. It may also say something about self-respect and responsibility.
11. Demonstrate reliability. This means, among other things, being punctual for meetings and following up promptly on items or information requested. It means, in essence, doing what you tell him you will do.

Although the key players are often very influential in custody disputes, they do not make the ultimate decision--that responsibility rests with the judge, subject of course to your right of appeal. Therefore, your challenge ultimately is to sell the judge on your case.

As a practical matter, key players hold special sway over certain judges. You must rely on your attorney to know his turf, to identify these relationships, and, where possible, to arrange the combination most helpful to your case. Obviously, this is not always possible. "Judge-shopping" is discouraged by various procedural constraints. However, your and your wife's lawyers will likely have considerable influence over the selection of key players, although, where their predilections are known, you will have considerable disagreement as well.

This leads me to a qualification of the tenets prescribed above for communicating with key players. If, for whatever reason, your attorney concludes that a certain key player is your implacable foe, you may take a more guarded, less communicative approach. In some cases, your attorney may want to be present at your meetings with this person. This is obviously a very difficult call requiring thoughtful assessment of the likely consequences, with the most predictable of these being further estrangement from the key player. This, of course, may be a lesser evil than the alternative, namely conscious collaboration with a known enemy.

Testifying at Trial

Despite the influence that a key player may or may not have, the judge is the final voice, subject of course to your right of appeal. Therefore, special attention must be given to the way you conduct yourself at trial.

Remember that your trial is the occasion when you and your spouse present all the most helpful facts and arguments to the judge. It is the culmination of all the time, money, and emotion you have invested in this great endeavor.

How you perform (for lack of a better word) on this occasion is a very influential factor in this outcome. Your challenge, as stated earlier, is to sell the judge on your case. This means you must testify. The judge will reach an opinion regarding your sincerity and credibility by all the ways that all of us use to judge the reliability of others' claims. Therefore, he will not only listen to your words, he will note your demeanor, your tone, and other nonverbal indicators of truthfulness.

Understanding how to testify effectively is not a difficult endeavor. With some special provisions, this is something you do in different contexts every day of your life.

Let me start by giving you some pointers on general courtroom decorum.

1. You are to stand when the judge enters and leaves the courtroom.

2. Do not talk when the judge is talking, irrespective of whether you are testifying.

3. If an objection is made by either counsel while you are testifying, stop talking immediately.

4. When testifying, speak clearly and with sufficient volume to ensure you are heard by everyone of importance in the courtroom.

5. When testifying, look regularly at the judge to let him know that you realize you are really talking to him.

6. Be well dressed and well groomed. You will never go wrong by wearing a suit to trial. A shave and haircut may be in order as well.

7. Be gentlemanly and courteous at all times, especially to opposing counsel.

8. Do not talk unless a question has been put to you.

You should also be concerned about how to conduct yourself when you are not on the stand. It is important to remember that the judge is likely observing you throughout the trial and not simply when you are on the stand. Therefore, at all times during the trial, behave like a gentleman. This point should be clear without further explanation, but experience has taught me otherwise. Here are a few suggestions:

1. Do not write and pass numerous and voluminous notes to your counsel during others' testimony. This distracts and annoys both your attorney and the judge.

2. Resist the temptation to demonstrate your opinion of a witness's testimony as he testifies. This means you should not demonstrate your anger or scorn by mumbling comments, making facial expressions, or exhibiting other body language.
3. Demonstrate interest and respect throughout the proceedings. Do not stare at the ceiling, slump in your chair, or doodle conspicuously.

4. Do not glare during the proceedings at the people in the courtroom that you do not like. The judge will notice this.

Now let us discuss what you do and say when you are in the witness box. This time can be divided into two basic categories: direct examination (when your attorney is asking you questions) and cross-examination (when the opposing attorney is asking you questions). This may occur in more than two segments. Each attorney may have a "redirect" and "recross," and you may be recalled to the stand.

I want to focus first and primarily on your cross-examination because this is the most troublesome phase for most clients. If you will recall the comments made in this chapter regarding how you should testify in a deposition, you will recall that the proceeding also consisted of cross-examination by opposing counsel (and possibly a guardian ad litem).

These guidelines apply to your testimony at trial, subject to a few very important exceptions. You may recall that regarding your deposition testimony, you were told not to "make argument." You were also told in that section to answer the questions as narrowly and succinctly as possible. Both of these rules, you will recall, are based on the fact that your challenge in your deposition is to reveal as little of your case as possible, while at the same time taking care to give enough information to answer the question. At your deposition, your primary audience was your opponent. Conversely, at trial, your audience is the person that will decide your and your children's future. Therefore, you must not miss any opportunity at trial to sell your case, including cross-examination.

This means that during your cross-examination at trial, unlike a deposition, you should attempt to powerfully state your case, advance your arguments where you can, liberally fill in helpful details, and offer exculpatory explanations when needed.

In other words, assume a more assertive style at trial. Having said all that, however, there is cause for some caution. Despite your objective to advance, or at least defend, your case on cross-examination, you must do so within the parameters of courtesy and crudity. Reread the rules in the preceding section for communicating with key people. Those principles will serve you well in all your testimony, whether during direct examination or cross-examination.

Additionally, review the deposition rules in Chapter 9. I would add the following rules for responding to cross-examination at trial:

1. Do not evade the question. This greatly annoys judges. Deal with the question asked, even if your answer is "I don't know." Then you may insert an explanatory or mitigating comment.

2. Although you want to get your point across, do not simply keep talking. Remember, the judge is wanting to get out on time. The ideal answer is brief but sufficiently explanatory.

3. A point made in the key player guidelines that bears repeating is that if you are asked about an incriminating and provable matter, do not attempt to run from it and do not equivocate. Step up to the plate. The net effect in the judge's mind may be a gain, that is, your credibility gain may outweigh your confessed shortcoming.

4. Do not feel that you have to recapture all your lost territory during the cross-examination itself. That is often impossible. What is worse about this overexpectant mentality is that you will end up coming off as combative and uncooperative. This may anger the judge. Besides, there is still time for redirect (your attorney's rebuttal). Remember, the primary purpose of redirect is to deal appropriately with damaging testimony on cross-examination. You must have some confidence in your attorney to help you clarify and explain.

5. In the deposition guidelines, which you have hopefully read, I discussed the leading question. The point of a leading question is to give the witness no room for any reply other

than yes or no, with heavy momentum toward a particular answer. Expect most of the questions put to you to take this form. This, however, does not mean that your reply must be one of two words. You have options: (1) If you do not know, say so and (2) if the technically correct answer is a yes or no, but it requires explanation, you can answer with a simple yes or no and then count on your attorney to clarify on redirect. This is risky for various reasons. The better policy in such cases is to simply give the full answer, incorporating the yes or no. Most judges will permit this so long as it is not long-winded and answers the question.

6. Although mentioned before, it bears repeating: do not allow the other attorney to bait you into anger, sarcasm, or other such unflattering reactions. Keep your cool throughout the questioning. In a divorce, a lot of such trigger topics exist. Expect offensive and embarrassing questions. Your testimony on direct examination will hopefully be entirely expected. Typically, your attorney will go over with you the subjects he intends to cover in your direct examination in advance of trial, including your anticipated answers. Ideally, this segment of the trial will unfold like a well-choreographed dance. The idea is to present a compelling and coherent picture. Although this cannot usually be done with your testimony alone, your testimony will nonetheless be a powerful element.

As a result, you need to know your steps. Your attorney is not allowed to "lead" you, as on cross-examination. You must know the answers. Know precisely what it is that you are being asked and why. Be sure you have mastered the information listed in the key player guidelines.

Your testimony on direct examination is your opportunity to

shine. Do your homework, rehearse your testimony with your attorney, and speak to the judge with respect and sincerity.

If you follow the rules set out in this chapter as to both conduct and communication throughout your divorce process, you will have a considerable advantage over most spouses in such cases. It is very easy to follow your emotions and to focus on unimportant things at the expense of critical issues. Hopefully, this chapter will prove a valuable road map to your intended destination.

10

Peace Talks: What if Settlement Is Reached?

There has never been
a protracted war from
which a country has benefited.

-Sun Tzu,
The Art of War,
circa 2000 BC

As previously mentioned, the parties are free to settle their case anytime they choose, as long as that time is before the conclusion of their trial, at which point the decision passes to the judge. Occasionally, cases are settled before either party even files a petition. At the other extreme, and far more common, are cases that settle on the day of trial, and some cases even settle during trial. Before going further, the term "settlement" may need some clarification. Technically, settlement simply means that both parties have agreed to certain terms that resolve their dispute. In this case these terms are, presumably, custody and related support issues. As already mentioned, settlements can be partial. You and your wife may resolve only some of the matters disputed, leaving others for trial.

In reality, the various issues in a divorce are usually overlapping.

This is simply the nature of negotiation. Let us assume that the only issues in your divorce are a house and custody. You happen to know that one of your wife's main concerns is to be able to continue living in the marital home after the divorce, yet it is unclear what the judge will do at trial. You, on the other hand, have moved into another place and are indifferent about the matter. Your main concern is getting a joint custody schedule that your wife opposes. Somewhere along the way, you can bet her lawyer will propose to your lawyer that you settle the property issue and simply hear the custody issue at trial. Are you going to do that? I bet not. You realize that if you insist on a package deal (all issues or none), you have more leverage to get what is important to you. Cynical, perhaps, but often effective.

Although a settlement by definition means agreement, this deal may not in fact be entirely consensual. It may be consensual in the sense that you may settle when Vito Corleone makes you an "offer you can't refuse." A settlement normally simply represents the intersection of each party's assessment of the best result that he or she can achieve at trial. Often these respective projections are based on fairly reliable information. Most influential, perhaps, are the judge's views as expressed in this and previous cases and, of course, the applicable law in your jurisdiction.

Not all cases settle for such rational reasons, however. Real-world factors, such as fear of embarrassing disclosures, lack of money for attorney's fees, and the hope of eventual reconciliation, may contribute more to a given deal than any calculus of probability.

Additionally, people prefer certainty. Unless the judge's position is known unequivocally, there is some level of uncertainty on both sides. For many clients, the risk, as well as the anxiety, of leaving the matter to the judge for decision is too much.

There are also factors of time and money to consider. In many jurisdictions, you will wait one to two years for your trial to wind its way down the docket. Meanwhile, both your and your wife's attorney's fees continue to climb. Depending on factors I will not get into here, you may be responsible for some portion of your wife's fees. Such fees normally increase dramatically as you approach your trial date.

What if you do make a deal with your spouse? Regarding the physical custodial arrangement, everything must be spelled out in detail. Do not assume any good faith will exist. If it does, great, but do not bet your and your kids' future on it. Handshakes mean nothing between divorcing spouses. Specify who picks up and drops off, the specific times, notification deadlines if someone is late, telephone contact, and so on.

TACTICAL INFORMATION 20

It is your reponsibility to scrutinize the provisions of your settlement agreement to ensure that it is free of gaps and ambiguities.

Regarding joint parenting issues, specify the duties and obligations of each parent as to the children's health care, education, religious training, and extracurricular activities. Typically, if one parent is awarded primary custody, that parent, at a minimum, has a duty to consult and confer with the other regarding such significant issues in the children's lives. Of course, if joint legal custody is awarded, greater cooperation is required. In either case, it is not enough to have these matters covered summarily in a few simple sentences. For such provisions to be enforceable, they must be sufficiently specific for a court to be able to hold the noncomplying party in contempt. Normally, such detail requires at least several paragraphs (see Appendix 5).

Similarly, support matters should be spelled out in comparable detail. Obviously, because of its quantitative nature, this subject easily lends itself to such precision. Furthermore, in virtually all states a panoply of legislative and administrative protections is automatically triggered when a child support order is given.

It is worth noting that the full police power of the state and federal governments has been harnessed to ensure money to moms, but there has been no corresponding interest shown to ensuring that dads have access to their kids. Therefore, if you are not being awarded primary custody, it is up to you to fastidiously scrutinize the provisions of your settlement agreement to ensure that it is free of gaps and ambiguities (see Appendix 5 for a sample agreement).

"If my wife and I do come to terms," clients commonly ask, "when is the deal binding? When is she locked in?" Let me begin by saying that oral agreements regarding these issues are almost universally unenforceable. In fact, courts are being progressive to the extent that they honor written agreements respecting children's welfare. I will try to put this in perspective. Put aside the issue of children for a minute and just think about spouses making deals. For the most part, courts allow people to enter into contracts between themselves to apportion their property as they choose. This is the free enterprise system at work. Although courts are fond of referring to marriage as a contract and therefore of applying contract principles where they can, this does have its limitations. Perhaps the most glaring of these is that the theoretical deal is likely driven more by passion than profit. Matters of the heart by definition do not lend themselves to rational calculation, as I am sure you can testify. Therefore, courts have historically viewed with suspicion deals made between spouses, be they an antenuptial agreement (one made before marriage) or a settlement agreement made before divorce. In both cases, the court has taken a paternalistic interest in assuring fairness. Antenuptial agreements in particular are legendary for their failure rate (a discussion of which can and has consumed volumes). Although settlement agreements are subject to different rules, they too can be set aside. The most common basis for doing so relates to "unconscionability" (when a court concludes that an agreement is grossly unfair).

To destabilize your deal even further, throw human beings into the mix. Keep in mind that the above discussion relates to agreements between spouses regarding property, money, and other such things. As you can probably imagine, if the court is solicitous regarding property in such cases, what do you anticipate will be the case when custody is being assigned? This is a whole new (and deeper) layer of concern. (I can hear the libertarian outcry as I write). The following statute from Missouri is a representative sample of state laws governing settlement agreements: Separation agreements authorized, effect of—orders for disposition of property, when—terms of agreement, how enforced.

§ 452.325.

1. To promote the amicable settlement of disputes between the parties to a marriage attendant upon their separation or the dissolution of their marriage, the parties may enter into a written separation agreement containing provisions for the maintenance of either of them, the disposition of any property owned by either of them, and the custody, support and visitation of their children.

2. In a proceeding for dissolution of marriage or for legal separation, the terms of the separation agreement, except terms providing for the custody, support, and visitation of children, are binding upon the court unless it finds, after considering the economic circumstances of the parties and any other relevant evidence produced by the parties, on their own motion or on request of the court, that the separation agreement is unconscionable.

3. If the court finds the separation agreement unconscionable, the court may request the parties to submit a revised separation agreement or the court may make orders for the disposition of property, support, and maintenance in accordance with the provisions of sections

452.330, 452.335 and 452.340.

4. If the court finds that the separation agreement is not unconscionable as to support, maintenance, and property:

(1) Unless the separation agreement provides to the contrary, its terms shall be set forth in the decree of dissolution or legal separation and the parties shall be ordered to perform them; or

(2) If the separation agreement provides that its terms shall not be set forth in the decree, only those terms concerning child support, custody and visitation shall be set forth in the decree, and the decree shall state that the court has found the remaining terms not unconscionable.

5. Terms of the agreement set forth in the decree are enforceable by all remedies available for the enforcement of a judgment. The court may punish any party who willfully violates its decree to the same extent as is provided by law for contempt of the court in any other suit or proceeding cognizable by the court.

6. Except for terms concerning the support, custody or visitation of children, the decree may expressly preclude or limit modification of terms set forth in the decree if the separation agreement so provides.

The statute inspires confidence in its first paragraph by telling spouses that they can make agreements regarding virtually all the issues in a divorce. Then in paragraphs 2 and 3, you find that the court can ignore the agreement if it finds it "unconscionable." What does this mean? No one knows for sure, not even the judges.

In paragraph 2, you find that any provisions relating to kids are completely unenforceable. "What good then," you are probably wondering, "is a settlement agreement relating to custody and support issues?" The answer may be "not much" if you are relying on it to bind the other party before your final hearing.

This statement often triggers the following question: will the judge at least know she made this deal, then backed out of it? My answer is a lawyerly yes and no. The judge will know of it if your attorney files a motion to enforce the settlement or if there is an argument over the award of attorney's fees that relates to work on the agreement. The matter may also come up in other appropriate discussions with the court.

However, the answer is no if your attorney seeks to offer the agreement as evidence of what your spouse really believes is good for your kids.

For public policy reasons, courts have long forbidden admitting into evidence settlement discussions between the parties. The fear is that no one would ever explore settlement if what he said was going to be repeated at a trial.

Therefore, such evidence may indeed be presented to the judge, but the judge may only consider it for certain permissible purposes, for instance, attorney's fees and enforceability, and not others. This is a fiction (technically speaking, of course).

11

Child Support: A Brief Discussion

In General

Regardless of the results of your fight to gain custody of your children, child support will be an issue in your case. In short, you will either be paying it or receiving it. Because money issues are the cause of substantial ill feelings between ex-spouses, and child support is at the top of many people's lists of money issues, it is a good idea to take a brief look at this topic.

Unlike the custody issue, courts have substantially less wiggle room ("discretion" in legal terminology) in setting the amount of child support to be paid. This is because, as a condition of receiving federal aid, the states are required to follow certain standards in their child support statutes. As a result, although the exact procedures and details vary from state to state, there is a certain basic pattern no matter where you live.

Generally, there will be a chart setting forth the base "presumed" amount of support to be paid. In making this determination, the chart will take into account income levels and the number of children to be supported. The chart support amounts are designed around the assumption that one parent will be the primary custodian who will have custody of the children the majority of the time.

There are a number of technical differences in exactly what numbers are plugged into the chart to arrive at the presumed support amount, depending on the particular state. Some states, e.g., Missouri, will plug gross income (before taxes) into the chart, and others, e.g., Texas, will use net income (after taxes). Many states use the combined income of both parties, e.g., Missouri, and then apportion the presumed support amount pro rata. Others use the income only of the party paying support, e.g., Illinois and Texas. In Texas, it gets even more complicated. Only the income of the party paying support is considered in the chart, but if that party has more than $6,000 per month in net (not gross) income, then both parties' income is considered in calculating additional support.

At least in theory, all the different variations on the chart should make no difference. The chart support amounts should be adjusted up or down to account for the source of the information being plugged in. In practice, however, the amounts vary from state to state. Furthermore, it is important to understand that the chart child support amount is not set only to meet the basic needs of the child. Rather, the child support amount increases as income levels increase, on the theory that the household in which the child lives should get a shot at approaching the standard of living the child would have had if the marriage had not ended.

After the chart support has been calculated, additional amounts are added in to account for the cost of day care and medical expenses. If the child has any extraordinary expenses, for instance, unusually high medical expenses, these may also be factored in the accounting. Finally, some states, e.g., Missouri, allow a downward adjustment to the presumed support to account, to a certain extent, for money spent during the time the party paying support has custody of the children. The result of all these calculations is the presumed child support amount.

Once the chart has been used to calculate the presumed support amount, if either party (payor or payee) wants to deviate from it, either up or down, that party has the burden of proving that the presumed support amount is unjust or inappropriate. This is generally not an easy task. "I have too many bills to pay that much support" is an insufficient reason. The judge will be looking for specific reasons, tailored to the needs of the child and not the needs of the payor, to justify ordering an amount other than chart support. Unless both parties agree to a different amount that the judge thinks is reasonable, most of the time chart support, or something close to it, is the end result.

One exception to this is the situation in which the physical custody of the children is split relatively evenly between Dad and Mom. In such a case, both parents are incurring expenses for the children at about the same rate. However, remember that the child support chart is designed around the assumption that one party will have custody of the children the majority of the time and, as a result, incur a majority of the children's expenses. As a result, where that assumption is false, the amount calculated pursuant to the chart may well be unjust and inappropriate. In fact, the Missouri child support laws specifically set forth this situation as one in which a deviation from chart support may be warranted.

If the judge is convinced that the presumed support amount is unjust or inappropriate, he then has fairly broad discretion to fashion an appropriate support order, taking into account factors such as the incomes and resources of the parties, the custody arrangements, extraordinary custodial expenses, and so forth.

After a support order is in place, the court may modify it on the showing of a substantial and continuing change in circumstances. What constitutes a "substantial and continuing change" is a judgment call, but a major change in the income of one or both parties qualifies. Another change that may not be so obvious is the children's increasing age. As children age, their expenses generally increase. As a result, it is quite possible for the recipient of child support to drag the payor back to court a few years later seeking more money.

TACTICAL INFORMATION 21

The party receiving support is presumed to spend the money on the children, and the burden is on the party paying to prove otherwise.

One question that dads frequently ask about a child support order is this: does Mom have to actually use the money to support the kids? After all, the amounts of support ordered pursuant to the chart can seem well in excess of the costs of the children's needs, and we all can picture situations in which, although the kids are not starving or neglected, Mom also has a nice new wardrobe courtesy of the support money. The answer is that, in general, the party receiving support is presumed to spend the money on the children, and the burden is on the party paying to prove otherwise. Because just about everyone paying support thinks they are paying too much, judges have a tendency to take a cynical view of parties coming into court with this kind of an issue. Furthermore, it is difficult to prove that expenditures do not benefit the children; for instance, if Mom buys a nice new house and uses some support money for it, that would benefit the kids, even if it benefits Mom more. As a result, it takes fairly direct evidence to get the party receiving support in trouble for not using it properly. Some states have statutes that can require the recipient of support to provide the payor with an accounting of where the support money went; it is difficult, however, to convince a judge to actually make this happen.

One issue that varies from state to state is the question of when support terminates. Although all states terminate support when the child dies, marries, enters the military, or becomes emancipated (self-supporting and living on his own), in the absence of these circumstances, the age at which support terminates varies. The majority of states allow child support to continue past the age of 18 (generally to the child's twenty-second birthday) if the child is attending college.

On the other hand, some states, such as Texas, terminate support when the child turns 18 unless he or she is still in high school.

Specific State Statutes

To understand how support works, it is helpful to examine the support statutes of a few large states. These are reproduced here in their entirety. They are not light reading but are nonetheless indispensable in demonstrating real-world applications of the principles set forth above.

Texas

Here are the basic support statutes for the state of Texas. Note that Texas determines the base child support amount by taking a percentage of the net income of the obligor (the person paying support) but only up to an income of $6,000 per month. Beyond that, proof of the children's actual expenses is required. This is unusual when compared with the statutes of most states. Texas terminates support at age 18, unless the child is still in high school.

§154.125 FAM. Application of Guidelines to Net Resources of $6,000 or Less

(a) The guidelines for the support of a child in this section are specifically designed to apply to situations in which the obligor's monthly net resources are $6,000 or less.

(b) If the obligor's monthly net resources are $6,000 or less, the court shall presumptively apply the following schedule in rendering the child support order:

Child Support Guidelines Based on the Monthly Net Resources of the Obligor

1 child: 20% of Obligor's Net Resources

2 children: 25% of Obligor's Net Resources

3 children: 30% of Obligor's Net Resources

4 children: 35% of Obligor's Net Resources

5 children: 40% of Obligor's Net Resources

6 + children: Not less than the amount for 5 children

Added by Acts 1995, 74th Leg., ch. 20, § 1, eff. April 20, 1995.

§154.126 FAM. Application of Guidelines to Net Resources of More Than $6,000 Monthly

(a) If the obligor's net resources exceed $6,000 per month, the court shall presumptively apply the percentage guidelines to the first $6,000 of the obligor's net resources. Without further reference to the percentage recommended by these guidelines, the court may order additional amounts of child support as appropriate, depending on the income of the parties and the proven needs of the child.

(b) The proper calculation of a child support order that exceeds the presumptive amount established for the first $6,000 of the obligor's net resources requires that the entire amount of the presumptive award be subtracted from the proven total needs of the child. After the presumptive award is subtracted, the court shall allocate between the parties the responsibility to meet the additional needs of the child according to the circumstances of the parties. However, in no event may the obligor be required to pay more child support than the greater of the presumptive amount or the amount equal to 100 percent of the proven needs of the child.

Added by Acts 1995, 74th Leg., ch. 20, 1, eff. April 20,

1995

§ 154.122 FAM. Application of Guidelines Rebuttably Presumed in Best Interest of Child

(a) The amount of a periodic child support payment established by the child support guidelines in effect in this state at the time of the hearing is presumed to be reasonable, and an order of support conforming to the guidelines is presumed to be in the best interest of the child.

(b) A court may determine that the application of the guidelines would be unjust or inappropriate under the circumstances.

Added by Acts 1995, 74th Leg., ch. 20, 1, eff. April 20, 1995.

§ 154.123 FAM. Additional Factors for Court to Consider

(a) The court may order periodic child support payments in an amount other than that established by the guidelines if the evidence rebuts the presumption that application of the guidelines is in the best interest of the child and justifies a variance from the guidelines.

(b) In determining whether application of the guidelines would be unjust or inappropriate under the circumstances, the court shall consider evidence of all relevant factors, including:

    (1) the age and needs of the child;

    (2) the ability of the parents to contribute to the support of the child;

    (3) any financial resources available for the support of the child;

(4) the amount of time of possession of and access to a child;

(5) the amount of the obligee's net resources, including the earning potential of the obligee if the actual income of the obligee is significantly less than what the obligee could earn because the obligee is intentionally unemployed or underemployed and including an increase or decrease in the income of the obligee or income that may be attributed to the property and assets of the obligee;

(6) child care expenses incurred by either party in order to maintain gainful employment;

(7) whether either party has the managing conservatorship or actual physical custody of another child;

(8) the amount of alimony or spousal maintenance actually and currently being paid or received by a party;

(9) the expenses for a son or daughter for education beyond secondary school;

(10) whether the obligor or obligee has an automobile, housing, or other benefits furnished by his or her employer, another person, or a business entity;

(11) the amount of other deductions from the wage or salary income and from other compensation for personal services of the parties;

(12) provision for health care insurance and payment of uninsured medical expenses;

(13) special or extraordinary educational, health care,

or other expenses of the parties or of the child;

(14) the cost of travel in order to exercise possession of and access to a child;

(15) positive or negative cash flow from any real and personal property and assets, including a business and investments;

(16) debts or debt service assumed by either party; and

(17) any other reason consistent with the best interest of the child, taking into consideration the circumstances of the parents.

Added by Acts 1995, 74th Leg., ch. 20, § 1, eff. April 20, 1995.

Florida

Here are Florida's child support statutes. Note that Florida actually includes the entire child support chart right in the statute. Although it is a bit long, it is reproduced here to give you an example of a support chart. In calculating support, Florida takes the combined net (not gross) income of both parties to determine a support amount from the chart and then allocates an amount pro rata to the paying party.

61.30 Child support guidelines; retroactive child support.

(1) (a) The child support guideline amount as determined by this section presumptively establishes the amount the trier of fact shall order as child support in an initial proceeding for such support or in a proceeding for modification of an existing order for such support, whether the proceeding arises under this or another chapter.

(b) The guidelines may provide the basis for proving a substantial change in circumstances upon which a

modification of an existing order may be granted. However, the difference between the existing monthly obligation and the amount provided for under the guidelines shall be at least 15 percent or $50, whichever amount is greater, before the court may find that the guidelines provide a substantial change in circumstances.

(c) In Title IV-D cases reviewed pursuant to the 3-year review and adjustment cycle, no change of circumstance need be proven to warrant a modification.

(2) Income shall be determined on a monthly basis for the obligor and for the obligee as follows:

(a) Gross income shall include, but is not limited to, the following items:

1. Salary or wages.
2. Bonuses, commissions, allowances, overtime, tips, and other similar payments.
3. Business income from sources such as self-employment, partnership, close corporations, and independent contracts. "Business income" means gross receipts minus ordinary and necessary expenses required to produce income.
4. Disability benefits.
5. Worker's compensation.
6. Unemployment compensation.
7. Pension, retirement, or annuity payments.
8. Social Security benefits.
9. Spousal support received from a previous

marriage or court ordered in the marriage before the court.

10. Interest and dividends.
11. Rental income, which is gross receipts minus ordinary and necessary expenses required to produce the income.
12. Income from royalties, trusts, or estates.
13. Reimbursed expenses or in kind payments to the extent that they educe living expenses.
14. Gains derived from dealings in property, unless the gain is nonrecurring.

(b) Income on a monthly basis shall be imputed to an unemployed or underemployed parent when such employment or underemployment is found to be voluntary on that parent's part, absent physical or mental incapacity or other circumstances over which the parent has no control. In the event of such voluntary unemployment or underemployment, the employment potential and probable earnings level of the parent shall be determined based upon his or her recent work history, occupational qualifications, and prevailing earnings level in the community. However, the court may refuse to impute income to a primary residential parent if the court finds it necessary for the parent to stay home with the child.

(c) Public assistance as defined in s. 409.2554 shall be excluded from gross income.

(3) Allowable deductions from gross income shall include:

(a) Federal, state, and local income tax deductions, adjusted for actual filing status and allowable dependents and income tax liabilities.

(b) Federal insurance contributions or self-employment tax.

(c) Mandatory union dues.

(d) Mandatory retirement payments.

(e) Health insurance payments, excluding payments for coverage of the minor child.

(f) Court-ordered support for other children which is actually paid.

(g) Spousal support paid pursuant to a court order from a previous marriage or the marriage before the court.

(4) Net income for the obligor and net income for the obligee shall be computed by subtracting allowable deductions from gross income.

(5) Net income for the obligor and net income for the obligee shall be added together for a combined net income.

(6) The following schedules shall be applied to the combined net income to determine the minimum child support need:

Combined Monthly Available	Child or Children					
Income	One	Two	Three	Four	Five	Six
650.00	74	75	75	76	77	78
700.00	119	120	121	123	124	125
750.00	164	166	167	169	171	173
800.00	190	211	213	216	218	220
850.00	202	257	259	262	265	268
900.00	213	302	305	309	312	315

Combined Monthly Available	Child or Children					
Income	One	Two	Three	Four	Five	Six
950.00	224	347	351	355	359	363
1000.00	235	365	397	402	406	410
1050.00	246	382	443	448	453	458
1100.00	258	400	489	495	500	505
1150.00	269	417	522	541	547	553
1200.00	280	435	544	588	594	600
1250.00	290	451	565	634	641	648
1300.00	300	467	584	659	688	695
1350.00	310	482	603	681	735	743
1400.00	320	498	623	702	765	790
1450.00	330	513	642	724	789	838
1500.00	340	529	662	746	813	869
1550.00	350	544	681	768	836	895
1600.00	360	560	701	790	860	920
1650.00	370	575	720	812	884	945
1700.00	380	591	740	833	907	971
1750.00	390	606	759	855	931	996
1800.00	400	622	779	877	955	1022
1850.00	410	638	798	900	979	1048
1900.00	421	654	818	923	1004	1074
1950.00	431	670	839	946	1029	1101
2000.00	442	686	859	968	1054	1128
2050.00	452	702	879	991	1079	1154

Combined Monthly Available Income	Child or Children					
	One	Two	Three	Four	Five	Six
2100.00	463	718	899	1014	1104	1181
2150.00	473	734	919	1037	1129	1207
2200.00	484	751	940	1060	1154	1234
2250.00	494	767	960	1082	1179	1261
2300.00	505	783	980	1105	1204	1287
2350.00	515	799	1000	1128	1229	1314
2400.00	526	815	1020	1151	1254	1340
2450.00	536	831	1041	1174	1279	1367
2500.00	547	847	1061	1196	1304	1394
2550.00	557	864	1081	1219	1329	1420
2600.00	568	880	1101	1242	1354	1447
2650.00	578	896	1121	1265	1379	1473
2700.00	588	912	1141	1287	1403	1500
2750.00	597	927	1160	1308	1426	1524
2800.00	607	941	1178	1328	1448	1549
2850.00	616	956	1197	1349	1471	1573
2900.00	626	971	1215	1370	1494	1598
2950.00	635	986	1234	1391	1517	1622
3000.00	644	1001	1252	1412	1540	1647
3050.00	654	1016	1271	1433	1563	1671
3100.00	663	1031	1289	1453	1586	1695
3150.00	673	1045	1308	1474	1608	1720
3200.00	682	1060	1327	1495	1631	1744

Combined Monthly Available	Child or Children					
Income	One	Two	Three	Four	Five	Six
3250.00	691	1075	1345	1516	1654	1769
3300.00	701	1090	1364	1537	1677	1793
3350.00	710	1105	1382	1558	1700	1818
3400.00	720	1120	1401	1579	1723	1842
3450.00	729	1135	1419	1599	1745	1867
3500.00	738	1149	1438	1620	1768	1891
3550.00	748	1164	1456	1641	1791	1915
3600.00	757	1179	1475	1662	1814	1940
3650.00	767	1194	1493	1683	1837	1964
3700.00	776	1208	1503	1702	1857	1987
3750.00	784	1221	1520	1721	1878	2009
3800.00	793	1234	1536	1740	1899	2031
3850.00	802	1248	1553	1759	1920	2053
3900.00	811	1261	1570	1778	1940	2075
3950.00	819	1275	1587	1797	1961	2097
4000.00	828	1288	1603	1816	1982	2119
4050.00	837	1302	1620	1835	2002	2141
4100.00	846	1315	1637	1854	2023	2163
4150.00	854	1329	1654	1873	2044	2185
4200.00	863	1342	1670	1892	2064	2207
4250.00	872	1355	1687	1911	2085	2229
4300.00	881	1369	1704	1930	2106	2251
4350.00	889	1382	1721	1949	2127	2273

Combined Monthly Available	Child or Children					
Income	One	Two	Three	Four	Five	Six
4400.00	898	1396	1737	1968	2147	2295
4450.00	907	1409	1754	1987	2168	2317
4500.00	916	1423	1771	2006	2189	2339
4550.00	924	1436	1788	2024	2209	2361
4600.00	933	1450	1804	2043	2230	2384
4650.00	942	1463	1821	2062	2251	2406
4700.00	951	1477	1838	2081	2271	2428
4750.00	959	1490	1855	2100	2292	2450
4800.00	968	1503	1871	2119	2313	2472
4850.00	977	1517	1888	2138	2334	2494
4900.00	986	1530	1905	2157	2354	2516
4950.00	993	1542	1927	2174	2372	2535
5000.00	1000	1551	1939	2188	2387	2551
5050.00	1006	1561	1952	2202	2402	2567
5100.00	1013	1571	1964	2215	2417	2583
5150.00	1019	1580	1976	2229	2432	2599
5200.00	1025	1590	1988	2243	2447	2615
5250.00	1032	1599	2000	2256	2462	2631
5300.00	1038	1609	2012	2270	2477	2647
5350.00	1045	1619	2024	2283	2492	2663
5400.00	1051	1628	2037	2297	2507	2679
5450.00	1057	1638	2049	2311	2522	2695
5500.00	1064	1647	2061	2324	2537	2711

Combined Monthly Available Income	Child or Children					
	One	Two	Three	Four	Five	Six
5550.00	1070	1657	2073	2338	2552	2727
5600.00	1077	1667	2085	2352	2567	2743
5650.00	1083	1676	2097	2365	2582	2759
5700.00	1089	1686	2109	2379	2597	2775
5750.00	1096	1695	2122	2393	2612	2791
5800.00	1102	1705	2134	2406	2627	2807
5850.00	1107	1713	2144	2418	2639	2820
5900.00	1111	1721	2155	2429	2651	2833
5950.00	1116	1729	2165	2440	2663	2847
6000.00	1121	1737	2175	2451	2676	2860
6050.00	1126	1746	2185	2462	2688	2874
6100.00	1131	1754	2196	2473	2700	2887
6150.00	1136	1762	2206	2484	2712	2900
6200.00	1141	1770	2216	2495	2724	2914
6250.00	1145	1778	2227	2506	2737	2927
6300.00	1150	1786	2237	2517	2749	2941
6350.00	1155	1795	2247	2529	2761	2954
6400.00	1160	1803	2258	2540	2773	2967
6450.00	1165	1811	2268	2551	2785	2981
6500.00	1170	1819	2278	2562	2798	2994
6550.00	1175	1827	2288	2573	2810	3008
6600.00	1179	1835	2299	2584	2822	3021
6650.00	1184	1843	2309	2595	2834	3034

Combined Monthly Available	Child or Children					
Income	One	Two	Three	Four	Five	Six
6700.00	1189	1850	2317	2604	2845	3045
6750.00	1193	1856	2325	2613	2854	3055
6800.00	1196	1862	2332	2621	2863	3064
6850.00	1200	1868	2340	2630	2872	3074
6900.00	1204	1873	2347	2639	2882	3084
6950.00	1208	1879	2355	2647	2891	3094
7000.00	1212	1885	2362	2656	2900	3103
7050.00	1216	1891	2370	2664	2909	3113
7100.00	1220	1897	2378	2673	2919	3123
7150.00	1224	1903	2385	2681	2928	3133
7200.00	1228	1909	2393	2690	2937	3142
7250.00	1232	1915	2400	2698	2946	3152
7300.00	1235	1921	2408	2707	2956	3162
7350.00	1239	1927	2415	2716	2965	3172
7400.00	1243	1933	2423	2724	2974	3181
7450.00	1247	1939	2430	2733	2983	3191
7500.00	1251	1945	2438	2741	2993	3201
7550.00	1255	1951	2446	2750	3002	3211
7600.00	1259	1957	2453	2758	3011	3220
7650.00	1263	1963	2461	2767	3020	3230
7700.00	1267	1969	2468	2775	3030	3240
7750.00	1271	1975	2476	2784	3039	3250
7800.00	1274	1981	2483	2792	3048	3259

Combined Monthly Available Income	Child or Children					
	One	Two	Three	Four	Five	Six
7850.00	1278	1987	2491	2801	3057	3269
7900.00	1282	1992	2498	2810	3067	3279
7950.00	1286	1998	2506	2818	3076	3289
8000.00	1290	2004	2513	2827	3085	3298
8050.00	1294	2010	2521	2835	3094	3308
8100.00	1298	2016	2529	2844	3104	3318
8150.00	1302	2022	2536	2852	3113	3328
8200.00	1306	2028	2544	2861	3122	3337
8250.00	1310	2034	2551	2869	3131	3347
8300.00	1313	2040	2559	2878	3141	3357
8350.00	1317	2046	2566	2887	3150	3367
8400.00	1321	2052	2574	2895	3159	3376
8450.00	1325	2058	2581	2904	3168	3386
8500.00	1329	2064	2589	2912	3178	3396
8550.00	1333	2070	2597	2921	3187	3406
8600.00	1337	2076	2604	2929	3196	3415
8650.00	1341	2082	2612	2938	3205	3425
8700.00	1345	2088	2619	2946	3215	3435
8750.00	1349	2094	2627	2955	3224	3445
8800.00	1352	2100	2634	2963	3233	3454
8850.00	1356	2106	2642	2972	3242	3464
8900.00	1360	2111	2649	2981	3252	3474
8950.00	1364	2117	2657	2989	3261	3484

Combined Monthly Available Income	Child or Children					
	One	Two	Three	Four	Five	Six
9000.00	1368	2123	2664	2998	3270	3493
9050.00	1372	2129	2672	3006	3279	3503
9100.00	1376	2135	2680	3015	3289	3513
9150.00	1380	2141	2687	3023	3298	3523
9200.00	1384	2147	2695	3032	3307	3532
9250.00	1388	2153	2702	3040	3316	3542
9300.00	1391	2159	2710	3049	3326	3552
9350.00	1395	2165	2717	3058	3335	3562
9400.00	1399	2171	2725	3066	3344	3571
9450.00	1403	2177	2732	3075	3353	3581
9500.00	1407	2183	2740	3083	3363	3591
9550.00	1411	2189	2748	3092	3372	3601
9600.00	1415	2195	2755	3100	3381	3610
9650.00	1419	2201	2763	3109	3390	3620
9700.00	1422	2206	2767	3115	3396	3628
9750.00	1425	2210	2772	3121	3402	3634
9800.00	1427	2213	2776	3126	3408	3641
9850.00	1430	2217	2781	3132	3414	3647
9900.00	1432	2221	2786	3137	3420	3653
9950.00	1435	2225	2791	3143	3426	3659
10000.00	1437	2228	2795	3148	3432	3666

For combined monthly available income less than the amount set out on the above schedules, the parent should be ordered to pay a child support amount, determined on a case-by-case basis. This will establish the principle of payment and lay the basis for increased orders should the parent's income increase in the future. For combined monthly available income greater than the amount set out in the above schedules, the obligation shall be the minimum amount of support provided by the guidelines plus the following percentages multiplied by the amount of income over $10,000:

Child or Children					
One	Two	Three	Four	Five	Six
5.0%	7.5%	9.5%	11.0%	12.0%	12.5%

(7) Child care costs incurred on behalf of the children due to employment, job search, or education calculated to result in employment or to enhance income of current employment of either parent shall be reduced by 25 percent and then shall be added to the basic obligation. After the adjusted child care costs are added to the basic obligation, any moneys prepaid by the noncustodial parent for child care costs for the child or children of this action shall be deducted from that noncustodial parent's child support obligation for that child or those children. Child care costs shall not exceed the level required to provide quality care from a licensed source for the children.

(8) Health insurance costs resulting from coverage ordered pursuant to s. 61.13(1)(b), and any noncovered medical, dental, and prescription medication expenses of the child,

shall be added to the basic obligation unless these expenses have been ordered to be separately paid on a percentage basis. After the health insurance costs are added to the basic obligation, any moneys prepaid by the noncustodial parent for health-related costs for the child or children of this action shall be deducted from that noncustodial parent's child support obligation for that child or those children.

(9) Each parent's percentage share of the child support need shall be determined by dividing each parent's net income by the combined net income.

(10) Each parent's actual dollar share of the child support need shall be determined by multiplying the minimum child support need by each parent's percentage share.

(11) The court may adjust the minimum child support award, or either or both parent's share of the minimum child support award, based upon the following considerations:

(a) Extraordinary medical, psychological, educational, or dental expenses.

(b) Independent income of the child, not to include moneys received by a child from supplemental security income.

(c) The payment of support for a parent which regularly has been paid and for which there is a demonstrated need.

(d) Seasonal variations in one or both parents' incomes or expenses.

(e) The age of the child, taking into account the greater needs of older children.

(f) Special needs, such as costs that may be associated

with the disability of a child, that have traditionally been met within the family budget even though the fulfilling of those needs will cause the support to exceed the proposed guidelines.

(g) The particular shared parental arrangement. For example, where the children spend a substantial amount of their time with the secondary residential parent (thereby reducing the financial expenditures incurred by the primary residential parent), or the secondary residential parent refuses to become involved in the activities of the child, or giving due consideration to the primary residential parent's homemaking services. If a child has visitation with a noncustodial parent for more than 28 consecutive days the court may reduce the amount of support paid to the custodial parent during the time of visitation not to exceed 50 percent of the amount awarded.

(h) Total available assets of the obligee, obligor, and the child.

(i) The impact of the Internal Revenue Service dependency exemption and waiver of that exemption. The court may order the primary residential parent to execute a waiver of the Internal Revenue Service dependency exemption if the noncustodial parent is current in support payments.

(j) When application of the child support guidelines requires a person to pay another person more than 55 percent of his or her gross income for a child support obligation for current support resulting from a single support order.

(k) Any other adjustment which is needed to achieve an equitable result which may include, but not be limited to, a reasonable and necessary existing expense or debt. Such expense or debt may include, but is not limited to, a reasonable and necessary expense or debt which the parties jointly incurred during the marriage.

(12) A parent with a support obligation may have other children living with him or her who were born or adopted after the support obligation arose. The existence of such subsequent children should not as a general rule be considered by the court as a basis for disregarding the amount provided in the guidelines. The parent with a support obligation for subsequent children may raise the existence of such subsequent children as a justification for deviation from the guidelines. However, if the existence of such subsequent children is raised, the income of the other parent of the subsequent children shall be considered by the court in determining whether or not there is a basis for deviation from the guideline amount. The issue of subsequent children may only be raised in a proceeding for an upward modification of an existing award and may not be applied to justify a decrease in an existing award.

(13) If the recurring income is not sufficient to meet the needs of the child, the court may order child support to be paid from nonrecurring income or assets.

(14) Every petition for child support or for modification of child support shall be accompanied by an affidavit which shows the party's income, allowable deductions, and net income computed in accordance with this section. The affidavit shall be served at the same time that the petition is served. The respondent, whether or not a stipulation is entered, shall make an affidavit which shows the party's income, allowable deductions, and net income computed in accordance with this section. The respondent shall include

his or her affidavit with the answer to the petition or as soon thereafter as is practicable, but in any case at least 72 hours prior to any hearing on the finances of either party.

(15) For purposes of establishing an obligation for support in accordance with this section, if a person who is receiving public assistance is found to be noncooperative as defined in s. 409.2572, the IV-D agency is authorized to submit to the court an affidavit attesting to the income of the custodial parent based upon information available to the IV-D agency.

(16) The Legislature shall review the guidelines established in this section at least every 4 years beginning in 1997.

(17) In an initial determination of child support, whether in a paternity action, dissolution of marriage action, or petition for support during the marriage, the court has discretion to award child support retroactive to the date when the parents did not reside together in the same household with the child, not to exceed a period of 24 months preceding the filing of the petition, regardless of whether that date precedes the filing of the petition. In determining the retroactive award in such cases, the court shall consider the following:

(a) The court shall apply the guidelines in effect at the time of the hearing subject to the obligor's demonstration of his or her actual income, as defined by subsection (2), during the retroactive period. Failure of the obligor to so demonstrate shall result in the court using the obligor's income at the time of the hearing in computing child support for the retroactive period.

(b) All actual payments made by the noncustodial parent to the custodial parent or the child or third parties for the benefit of the child throughout the proposed retroactive period.

(c) The court should consider an installment payment plan for the payment of retroactive child support.

California

California, unlike many states, does not use a chart of support amounts. Rather, California uses a formula based on percentages of both parties' net income to come up with a presumed support amount. The formula demonstrates the benefit of using a chart in that it is almost incomprehensible without a strong algebra background. Here is California's method for calculating child support.

§4055 Fam.

(a) The statewide uniform guideline for determining child support orders is as follows: CS = K (HN - (H%) (TN)).

(b) (1) The components of the formula are as follows:

(a) CS = child support amount.

(b) K = amount of both parents' income to be allocated for child support as set forth in paragraph.

(c) HN = high earner's net monthly disposable income.

(d) H% = approximate percentage of time that the high earner has or will have primary physical responsibility for the children compared to the other parent. In cases in which parents have different time-sharing arrangements for different children, H% equals the average of the approximate percentages of time the high earner parent spends with each child.

(e) TN = total net monthly disposable income of both parties.

(2) To compute net disposable income, see Section 4059.

(3) K (amount of both parents' income allocated for child support) equals one plus H% (if H% is less than or equal to 50 percent) or two minus H% (if H% is greater than 50 percent) times the following fraction:

Total Net Disposable Income Per Month	K
$0-800	0.20 + TN/16,000
$801-6,666	0.25
$6,667-10,000	0.10 + 1,000/TN
Over $10,000	0.12 + 800/TN

For example, if H% equals 20 percent and the total monthly net disposable income of the parents is $1,000, K = (1 + 0.20) x 0.25, or 0.30. If H% equals 80 percent and the total monthly net disposable income of the parents is $1,000, K = (2 - 0.80) x 0.25, or 0.30.

(4) For more than one child, multiply CS by:	
2 children	1.6
3 children	2
4 children	2.3
5 children	2.5
6 children	2.625
7 children	2.75
8 children	2.813
9 children	2.844
10 children	2.86

(5) If the amount calculated under the formula results in a positive number, the higher earner shall pay that amount to the lower earner. If the amount calculated under the formula results in a negative number, the lower earner shall pay the absolute value of that amount to the higher earner.

(6) In any default proceeding where proof is by affidavit pursuant to Section 2336, or in any proceeding for child support in which a party fails to appear after being duly noticed, H% shall be set at zero in the formula if the noncustodial parent is the higher earner or at 100 if the custodial parent is the higher earner, where there is no evidence presented demonstrating the percentage of time that the noncustodial parent has primary physical responsibility for the children. H% shall not be set as described above if the moving party in a default proceeding is the noncustodial parent or if the party who fails to appear after being duly noticed is the custodial parent. A statement by the party who is not in default as to the percentage of time that the noncustodial parent has primary physical responsibility for the children shall be deemed sufficient evidence.

(7) In all cases in which the net disposable income per month of the obligor is less than one thousand dollars ($1,000), the court shall rule on whether a low-income adjustment shall be made. The ruling shall be based on the facts presented to the court, the principles provided in Section 4053, and the impact of the contemplated adjustment on the respective net incomes of the obligor and the obligee. Where the court has ruled that a low-income adjustment shall be made, the child support amount otherwise determined under this section shall be

reduced by an amount that is no greater than the amount calculated by multiplying the child support amount otherwise determined under this section by a fraction, the numerator of which is 1,000 minus the obligor's net disposable income per month, and the denominator of which is 1,000. If a low-income adjustment is allowed, the court shall state the reasons supporting the adjustment in writing or on the record and shall document the amount of the adjustment and the underlying facts and circumstances.

(8) Unless the court orders otherwise, the order for child support shall allocate the support amount so that the amount of support for the youngest child is the amount of support for one child, and the amount for the next youngest child is the difference between that amount and the amount for two children, with similar allocations for additional children. However, this paragraph does not apply to cases in which there are different time-sharing arrangements for different children or where the court determines that the allocation would be inappropriate in the particular case.

(c) If a court uses a computer to calculate the child support order, the computer program shall not automatically default affirmatively or negatively on whether a low-income adjustment is to be applied. If the low-income adjustment is applied, the computer program shall not provide the amount of the low-income adjustment. Instead, the computer program shall ask the user whether or not to apply the low-income adjustment, and if answered affirmatively, the computer program shall provide the range of the adjustment permitted by paragraph (7) of subdivision (b).

(Amended by Stats. 1998, Ch. 581, Sec. 15. Effective January 1,1999.)

§ 4057 Fam.

(a) The amount of child support established by the formula provided in subdivision (a) of Section 4055 is presumed to be the correct amount of child support to be ordered.

(b) The presumption of subdivision (a) is a refutable presumption affecting the burden of proof and may be rebutted by admissible evidence showing that application of the formula would be unjust or inappropriate in the particular case, consistent with the principles set forth in Section 4053, because one or more of the following factors is found to be applicable by a preponderance of the evidence, and the court states in writing or on the record the information required in subdivision (a) of Section 4056:

(1) The parties have stipulated to a different amount of child support under subdivision (a) of Section 4065.

(2) The sale of the family residence is deferred pursuant to Chapter 8 (commencing with Section 3800) of Part 1 and the rental value of the family residence in which the children reside exceeds the mortgage payments, homeowner's insurance, and property taxes. The amount of any adjustment pursuant to this paragraph shall not be greater than the excess amount.

(3) The parent being ordered to pay child support has an extraordinarily high income and the amount determined under the formula would exceed the needs of the children.

(4) A party is not contributing to the needs of the children at a level commensurate with that party's custodial time.

(5) Application of the formula would be unjust or inappropriate due to special circumstances in the particular case. These special circumstances include, but are not limited to, the following:

(a) Cases in which the parents have different time-sharing arrangements for different children.

(b) Cases in which both parents have substantially equal time-sharing of the children and one parent has a much lower or higher percentage of income used for housing than the other parent.

(c) Cases in which the children have special medical or other needs that could require child support that would be greater than the formula amount.

(Amended (as added by Stats. 1993, Ch. 219, Sec. 138) by Stats. 1993, Ch. 1156, Sec. 3.5. Effective January 1, 1994.)

New York

Here are the New York child support statutes. New York calculates support by taking a percentage of the combined income of the parties (the exact percentage depends on the number of children) and then allocating it pro rata. Unlike most states, New York does not use either gross or net income in this calculation; rather, it takes gross income less certain expenses, including federal social security (FICA) taxes but not federal income tax.

§240 Dom. Rel. Custody and child support; orders of protection.

(sections omitted)

1-b.

(a) The court shall make its award for child support pursuant to the provisions of this subdivision. The court

may vary from the amount of the basic child support obligation determined pursuant to paragraph (c) of this subdivision only in accordance with paragraph (f) of this subdivision.

(b) For purposes of this subdivision, the following definitions shall be used:

(1) "Basic child support obligation" shall mean the sum derived by adding the amounts determined by the application of subparagraphs two and three of paragraph (c) of this subdivision except as increased pursuant to subparagraphs four, five, six and seven of such paragraph.

(2) "Child support" shall mean a sum to be paid pursuant to court order or decree by either or both parents or pursuant to a valid agreement between the parties for care, maintenance and education of any unemancipated child under the age of twenty-one years.

(3) "Child support percentage" shall mean:

(i) seventeen percent of the combined parental income for one child;

(ii) twenty-five percent of the combined parental income for two children;

(iii) twenty-nine percent of the combined parental income for three children;

(iv) thirty-one percent of the combined parental income for four children; and

(v) no less than thirty-five percent of the combined parental income for five or more children.

(4) "Combined parental income" shall mean the sum of the income of both parents.

(5) "Income" shall mean, but shall not be limited to, the sum of the amounts determined by the application of clauses (I), (ii), (iii), (iv), (v) and (vi) of this subparagraph reduced by the amount determined by the application of clause (vii) of this subparagraph:

(i) gross (total) income as should have been or should be reported in the most recent federal income tax return. If an individual files his/her federal income tax return as a married person filing jointly, such person shall be required to prepare a form, sworn to under penalty of law, disclosing his/her gross income individually;

(ii) to the extent not already included in gross income in clause (I) of this subparagraph, investment income reduced by sums expended in connection with such investment;

(iii) to the extent not already included in gross income in clauses (I) and (ii) of this subparagraph, the amount of income or compensation voluntarily deferred and income received, if any, from the following sources:

(A) workers' compensation,

(B) disability benefits,

(C) unemployment insurance benefits,

(D) social security benefits,

(E) veterans benefits,

(F) pensions and retirement benefits,

(G) fellowships and stipends, and

(H) annuity payments;

(iv) at the discretion of the court, the court may attribute or impute income from, such other resources as may be available to the parent, including, but not limited to:

(A) non-income producing assets,

(B) meals, lodging, memberships, automobiles or other perquisites that are provided as part of compensation for employment to the extent that such perquisites constitute expenditures for personal use, or which expenditures directly or indirectly confer personal economic benefits,

(C) fringe benefits provided as part of compensation for employment, and

(D) money, goods, or services provided by relatives and friends;

(v) an amount imputed as income based upon the parent's former resources or income, if the court determines that a parent has reduced resources or income in order to reduce or avoid the parent's obligation for child support;

(vi) to the extent not already included in gross income in clauses (I) and (ii) of this subparagraph, the following self-employment deductions attributable to self-employment carried on by the taxpayer:

(a) any depreciation deduction greater than depreciation calculated on a straight-line basis for the purpose of determining business income or investment credits, and

(b) entertainment and travel allowances deducted from business income to the extent said allowances reduce personal expenditures;

(vii) the following shall be deducted from income prior to applying the provisions of paragraph (c) of this subdivision:

(a) unreimbursed employee business expenses except to the extent said expenses reduce personal expenditures,

(b) alimony or maintenance actually paid to a spouse not a party to the instant action pursuant to court order or validly executed written agreement,

(c) alimony or maintenance actually paid or to be paid to a spouse that is a party to the instant action pursuant to an existing court order or contained in the order to be entered by the court, or pursuant to a validly executed written agreement, provided the order or agreement provides for a specific adjustment, in accordance with this subdivision, in the amount of child support payable upon the termination of alimony or maintenance to such spouse,

(d) child support actually paid pursuant to court order or written agreement on behalf of any child for whom the parent has a legal duty of support and who is not subject to the instant action,

(e) public assistance,

(f) supplemental security income,

(g) New York City or Yonkers income or earnings taxes actually paid, and

(h) Federal Insurance Contributions Act (FICA) taxes actually paid.

(6) "Self-support reserve" shall mean one hundred thirty-five percent of the poverty income guidelines amount for a single person as reported by the federal Department of Health and Human services. For the calendar year nineteen hundred eighty-nine, the self-support reserve shall be eight thousand sixty-five dollars. On March first of each year, the self-support reserve shall be revised to reflect the annual updating of the poverty income guidelines as reported by the federal Department of Health and Human

Services for a single person household.

(c) The amount of the basic child support obligation shall be determined in accordance with the provision of this paragraph:

(1) The court shall determine the combined parental income.

(2) The court shall multiply the combined parental income up to eighty thousand dollars by the appropriate child support percentage and such amount shall be prorated in the same proportion as each parent's income is to the combined parental income.

(3) Where the combined parental income exceeds the dollar amount set forth in subparagraph two of this paragraph, the court shall determine the amount of child support for the amount of the combined parental income in excess of such dollar amount through consideration of the factors set forth in paragraph (f) of this subdivision and/or the child support percentage.

(4) Where the custodial parent is working, or receiving elementary or secondary education, or higher education or vocational training which the court determines will lead to employment, and incurs child care expenses as a result thereof, the court shall determine reasonable child care expenses and such child care expenses, where incurred, shall be prorated in the same proportion as each parent's income is to the combined parental income. Each parent's pro rata share of the child care expenses shall be separately stated and added to the sum of subparagraphs two and three of this paragraph.

(5) The court shall prorate each parent's share of future reasonable health care expenses of the child not covered by

insurance in the same proportion as each parent's income is to the combined parental income. The non-custodial parent's pro rata share of such health care expenses shall be paid in a manner determined by the court, including direct payment to the health care provider.

(6) Where the court determines that the custodial parent is seeking work and incurs child care expenses as a result thereof, the court may determine reasonable child care expenses and may apportion the same between the custodial and non-custodial parent. The non-custodial parent's share of such expenses shall be separately stated and paid in a manner determined by the court.

(7) Where the court determines, having regard for the circumstances of the case and of the respective parties and in the best interests of the child, and as justice requires, that the present or future provision of post-secondary, private, special, or enriched education for the child is appropriate, the court may award educational expenses. The non-custodial parent shall pay educational expenses, as awarded, in a manner determined by the court, including direct payment to the educational provider.

(d) Notwithstanding the provisions of paragraph (c) of this subdivision, where the annual amount of the basic child support obligation would reduce the non-custodial parent's income below the poverty income guidelines amount for a single person as reported by the federal Department of Health and Human Services, the basic child support obligation shall be twenty-five dollars per month or the difference between the non-custodial parent's income and the self-support reserve, whichever is greater. Notwithstanding the provisions of paragraph (c) of this subdivision, where the annual amount of the basic child support obligation would reduce the non-custodial parent's income below the self-support reserve but not below the poverty income guidelines amount for a single person as reported by the federal Department of Health and Human Services, the basic child support obligation shall be fifty dollars per month or the difference between the non-custodial parent's income and the self-support reserve, whichever is greater.

(e) Where a parent is or may be entitled to receive non-recurring payments from extraordinary sources not otherwise considered as income pursuant to this section, including but not limited to:

(1) Life insurance policies;

(2) Discharges of indebtedness;

(3) Recovery of bad debts and delinquency amounts;

(4) Gifts and inheritances; and

(5) Lottery winnings, the court, in accordance with paragraphs (c), (d) and (f) of this subdivision may allocate a proportion of the same to child support, and such amount shall be paid in a manner determined by the court.

(f) The court shall calculate the basic child support obligation, and the non-custodial parent's pro rata share of the basic child support obligation. Unless the court finds that the non-custodial parent's pro-rata share of the basic child support obligation is unjust or inappropriate, which finding shall be based upon consideration of the following factors:

(1) The financial resources of the custodial and non-custodial parent, and those of the child;

(2) The physical and emotional health of the child and his/her special needs and aptitudes;

(3) The standard of living the child would have enjoyed had the marriage or household not been dissolved;

(4) The tax consequences to the parties;

(5) The non-monetary contributions that the parents will make toward the care and well-being of the child;

(6) The educational needs of either parent;

(7) A determination that the gross income of one parent is substantially less than the other parent's gross income;

(8) The needs of the children of the non-custodial parent for whom the non-custodial parent is providing support who are not subject to the instant action and whose support has not been deducted from income pursuant to subclause (D) of clause (vii) of subparagraph five of paragraph (b) of this subdivision, and the financial resources of any person obligated to support such children, provided, however, that this factor may apply only if the resources available to support such children are less than the resources available to support the children who are subject to the instant action;

(9) Provided that the child is not on public assistance (I) extraordinary expenses incurred by the non-custodial parent in exercising visitation, or (ii) expenses incurred by the non-custodial parent in extended visitation provided that the custodial parent's expenses are substantially reduced as a result thereof; and

(10) Any other factors the court determines are relevant in each case, the court shall order the non-custodial parent to pay his or her pro rata share of the basic child support

obligation, and may order the non-custodial parent to pay an amount pursuant to paragraph (e) of this subdivision.

(g) Where the court finds that the non-custodial parent's pro rata share of the basic child support obligation is unjust or inappropriate, the court shall order the non-custodial parent to pay such amount of child support as the court finds just and appropriate, and the court shall set forth, in a written order, the factors it considered; the amount of each party's pro rata share of the basic child support obligation; and the reasons that the court did not order the basic child support obligation. Such written order may not be waived by either party or counsel; provided, however, and notwithstanding any other provision of law, the court shall not find that the non-custodial parent's pro rata share of such obligation is unjust or inappropriate on the basis that such share exceeds the portion of a public assistance grant which is attributable to a child or children. In no instance shall the court order child support below twenty-five dollars per month. Where the non-custodial parent's income is less than or equal to the poverty income guidelines amount for a single person as reported by the federal department of health and human services, unpaid child support arrears in excess of five hundred dollars shall not accrue.

(h) A validly executed agreement or stipulation voluntarily entered into between the parties after the effective date of this subdivision presented to the court for incorporation in an order or judgment shall include a provision stating that the parties have been advised of the provisions of this subdivision, and that the basic child support obligation provided for therein would presumptively result in the correct amount of child support to be awarded. In the event

that such agreement or stipulation deviates from the basic child support obligation, the agreement or stipulation must specify the amount that such basic child support obligation would have been and the reason or reasons that such agreement or stipulation does not provide for payment of that amount. Such provision may not be waived by either party or counsel. Nothing contained in this subdivision shall be construed to alter the rights of the parties to voluntarily enter into validly executed agreements or stipulations which deviate from the basic child support obligation provided such agreements or stipulations comply with the provisions of this paragraph. The court shall, however, retain discretion with respect to child support pursuant to this section. Any court order or judgment incorporating a validly executed agreement or stipulation which deviates from the basic child support obligation shall set forth the court's reasons for such deviation.

(i) Where either or both parties are unrepresented, the court shall not enter an order or judgment other than a temporary order pursuant to section two hundred thirty-seven of this article, that includes a provision for child support unless the unrepresented party or parties have received a copy of the child support standards chart promulgated by the commissioner of social services pursuant to subdivision two of section one hundred eleven-I of the social services law. Where either party is in receipt of child support enforcement services through the local social services district, the local social services district child support enforcement unit shall advise such party of the amount derived from application of the child support percentage and that such amount serves as a starting point

for the determination of the child support award, and shall provide such party with a copy of the child support standards chart. In no instance shall the court approve any voluntary support agreement or compromise that includes an amount for child support less than twenty-five dollars per month.

(j) In addition to financial disclosure required in section two hundred thirty-six of this article, the court may require that the income and/or expenses of either party be verified with documentation including, but not limited to, past and present income tax returns, employer statements, pay stubs, corporate, business, or partnership guides and records, corporate and business tax returns, and receipts for expenses or such other means of verification as the court determines appropriate. Nothing herein shall affect any party's right to pursue discovery pursuant to this chapter, the civil practice law and rules, or the family court act.

(k) When a party has defaulted and/or the court is otherwise presented with insufficient evidence to determine gross income, the court shall order child support based upon the needs or standard of living of the child, whichever is greater. Such order may be retroactively modified upward, without a showing of change in circumstances.

(l) In any action or proceeding for modification of an order of child support existing prior to the effective date of this paragraph, brought pursuant to this article, the child support standards set forth in this subdivision shall not constitute a change of circumstances warranting modification of such support order; provided, however, that

(1) where the circumstances warrant modification of such order, or (2) where any party objects to an adjusted child support order made or proposed at the direction of the support collection unit pursuant to section one hundred eleven-h or one hundred eleven-n of the social services law, and the court is reviewing the current order of child support, such standards shall be applied by the court in its determination with regard to the request for modification, or disposition of an objection to an adjusted child support order made or proposed by a support collection unit. In applying such standards, when the order to be modified incorporates by reference or merges with a validly executed separation agreement or stipulation of settlement, the court may consider, in addition to the factors set forth in paragraph (f) of this subdivision, the provisions of such agreement or stipulation concerning property distribution, distributive award and/or maintenance in determining whether the amount calculated by using the standards would be unjust or inappropriate.

12

After the Battle: Post-Divorce Issues

> The crisis, through which we are now passing, may leave us a wiser and better people, the teachings of adversity may enable us more fully to appreciate the blessings of prosperity.
>
> *-Sketches from the Seat of War: Civil War Letters of a Jewish Soldier*

What if you are already divorced, and your wife has primary custody of your kids? What if you became embroiled in an ugly custody dispute, you fought the good fight, but you lost? Is this the end of the story? In a word, no.

Robert E. Lee stands as one of America's greatest generals largely because he knew that discretion is the better part of valor. He understood the importance of preserving resources for that eventual occasion when the enemy, with otherwise superior firepower, is vulnerable. A more swaggering and less thoughtful approach from the leader of a weaker army facing a stronger foe would have reduced the Civil War to a few major battles.

Some men are similarly situated before, during, or after divorce. Through no fault of their own, the evidence is simply not there to win primary custody. In such a situation, a key decision must be made: do you recklessly charge forward in a blaze of glory (Lee did this once at Antietam), or do you settle along the best lines possible and begin positioning yourself for the next engagement?

Before going further, you should understand something about how a custody order is changed. In most states, this change order is called a "modification." Technically, a modification can be pursued at any time after the last order. However, even if he thinks a modification would be in the children's best interest, to request a modification, the party seeking the change (technically referred to as the "movant") generally has the burden of showing a "substantial change of circumstances" from the time of entry of the original order.

Although the specific language referring to the "change of circumstances" test varies from state to state, the purpose is always the same: after a divorce is concluded, the court system cannot permit one or both parties to subject the judicial system, the other party, and the children to a repetition of the first trial when there have been no significant new developments. This standard makes sense. I can tell you as a divorce lawyer that if such a standard did not exist, at least one of the parties in most divorces would come back the next day for another bite of the apple.

Given the above concerns, you will not be surprised to read that although you could theoretically have a "substantial change of circumstances" within six months of your divorce, as a practical matter, motions filed soon thereafter are viewed with suspicion. In fact, in some states the burden is expressly greater if you file a motion to modify within one year of the divorce.

Subject to this significant limitation, however, virtually all issues relating to the children, both custodial and financial, are subject to modification. Obviously, this must be true. Whatever the circumstances of the children and the parties at the time of the divorce, things change, and the unforeseeable occurs. The court must have a mechanism with which to deal with these changes. This is the reason for modification actions.

Returning to the Lee at Antietam conundrum, admittedly the reckless charge has a kind of heroic appeal to commend it. There is, of course, the possibility that you will win by an act of God or your opponent's timidity. The downside of this strategy is its tremendous cost. Unless you have lavish funds available, the $15,000 you spend on a modification fight will effect your potential for success in future, more auspicious, circumstances. For most people, funds are finite and must be intelligently rationed.

Another probably more important downside is the bad blood created, which may reduce your opportunities to strengthen your position in the future. Clearly, your decision regarding this question will depend on what you perceive to be the momentum of events. What is going on in your wife's life? What do you anticipate her situation to be over the next year?

I am willing to wager that if you are getting divorced, your wife has a boyfriend. She may be in her 30s and feeling a compulsion to give attention to her romantic and social life. She will be driven by a sense of urgency that you are not likely to feel. That will affect her priorities. Although she loves the kids, she has an inexhaustible supply of self-justification to fuel her various pursuits.

This trend may not be apparent to a court at the time of the divorce, although you may foresee it. As a result, the passage of time after the divorce provides both a record and an opportunity. It provides a record in that after the divorce, your ex will likely be indiscreet in her affairs (e.g., her activities, lifestyle, and resulting dependence on others to watch the kids). This is an opportunity if, during this time, you not only fastidiously exercise all the custodial time afforded you by your decree but also volunteer to assist on those other occasions.

This supplemental time would be but a fanciful wish to those dads emerging from a bitter but unsuccessful battle for primary custody. For others, however, the prospect is not so improbable. If you are capable of the self-restraint and diplomacy necessary to maintain detente with your former spouse, you can dramatically improve your position. You will likely be vouchsafed both custodial time and information not otherwise obtainable.

If you decide to come back and file another day, you should have a strategy calculated to improve your relative position over time. A "substantial change" may occur with respect to your circumstances, your wife's circumstances, or both. I suggest that you consider both sides of the scales-attend to your circumstances and pay attention to those of your ex.

If you defer the custody battle to a point in the future, there are some cardinal rules you must follow:

- Always stay current on child support payments, including indirect payments (e.g., for health care and day care). Make all such payments through an intermediary if possible to adequately document both the fact and time of payments; most states provide for wage assignments and/or payment through the court system. Remember, the burden of proving payment will be on you.
- Always exercise all the time afforded you in your decree. Do not blow off any weekends, summer weeks, or holidays.
- Participate as fully as your decree permits in decisions affecting your kids' health, education, and welfare. Initiate communications with teachers, doctors, counselors, and other key players.
- Always demonstrate a willingness to include the other parent as a co-parent. Inform mom of important incidents relating to your child's health, education, and welfare occurring while your child is in your care.
- Do not argue with your ex in front of the kids. Do not send

threatening letters. Do not disparage your ex in front of the kids.

- Be mindful of the suitability of your residence for primary custody; stability, a good neighborhood, and a good school system are influential. Be mindful of the suitability of your employment for primary custody; commuting time, travel, and work schedule are influential.
- Control your new wife. New wives can be deal killers in modification actions. They tend to be notoriously confrontational with Mom, reckless in their remarks in the kids' presence, and enthusiastically usurious of Mom's authority. Ironically, stepmoms are often the moving force behind dad's motion to modify. I brace myself for stepmom issues in the litigation when the new wife accompanies Dad to my office and dominates the discussion throughout the meeting.
- Document all matters relating to your kids. Be sure you are doing this at your attorney's behest so that it may be privileged and therefore nondiscoverable by the other side in a subsequent action. Specifically, document every time you have additional time with your kids, and when they are left in the care of others. Also, document communications with Mom. When Mom screws up, note it. This journal exercise should be brief, no more than 5 to 10 minutes a day. Remember, the judge probably did not endure "War and Peace" from cover to cover, so do not expect to succeed where Tolstoy failed.
- Leave the kids out of it. Do not drill the kids about what is going on in Mom's house. Do not attempt to win over the kids by criticizing Mom. If the kids volunteer information, that is fine, but do not solicit such alignment. At the risk of sounding naive, if you do the right thing, chances are your kids will too when the time comes.

What if your ex-wife refuses to follow the decree despite your charm, patience, and diplomacy? What if, despite your winsome and cooperative ways, your ex tampers with your rightful role in your kids' lives?

TACTICAL INFORMATION 22

To be found guilty of contempt, the court must conclude that the party acted deliberately and without good reason.

Whether these intrusions commence as border incidents or full-scale invasions, you cannot ignore them. Sometimes there are more important things than peace. After attempting to resolve the matter amicably by correspondence, a full retaliatory strike may be appropriate. Unless an overriding health or safety issue exists, pause only long enough to ensure that a solid record of the trespasses exists.

Bear in mind, however, that when in doubt, it is better to feign a determination to fix things amicably than to precipitously plunge into court with comparatively minor and premature complaints. The court's sympathy may lie on the other side of the courtroom when you jump the gun or are otherwise perceived as reactionary.

Regarding the legal enforcement mechanism, when a court order exists, the remedy for its violation is the filing of a motion for contempt (usually civil contempt) by the other party. Technically, a contempt action is appropriate anytime a party "contemptuously" violates any provision of the decree. As a practical matter, however, the violation or violations should be significant.

Remember that to be found guilty of contempt, it is not enough for the court to conclude that the accused party did not act in accordance with the decree. The court must also conclude that the accused party did so deliberately and without good reason. Your burden in most states is simply to show that Mom did not comply with the temporary custody, consulting with Dad on issues regarding the children, or any other provisions of the court order. It is then up to mom to present evidence that she did not have the ability to comply or that it was an "honest mistake." Often a motion for contempt will be filed in tandem with a motion to modify. If the contempt motion is well taken, this approach can position the other party in the court's mind, put them on the defensive, and enhance the credibility of your modification claims.

If you succeed in proving your case for contempt, the court has a whole range of remedies that you can request, ranging from incarceration to attorney's fees to compensatory custody time to other more customized remedies. Contempt can be a very powerful tool if the evidence is there.

13

Postscript

A dad facing divorce has a lot to consider. What should be clear is that when considering custody matters, your decisions are based largely (if not entirely) on emotional almost intuitive factors that cannot be reduced to simple math.

This is untrue of the other matters you must deal with in your divorce because everything else is financial (e.g., debts, assets, and maintenance). Although forecasts regarding such matters may be difficult, they are nonetheless numerical.

With regard to your children, however, the decision-making process is less clean. Your objective, as you know, is to do the best thing possible for your kids. That is an easy statement to make, but what exactly does it mean for your children? What is "best" and what is "possible"?

To answer these questions, you have to think about a host of factors already discussed. You have to weigh these intangible, often gray factors and make the right call.

Having said that, I want to emphasize this point in closing. Much has been said in this book about the torrent of emotions accompanying divorce from anger to anxiety to depression. Yet despite these potentially crippling influences on your judgment, you cannot simply call in sick, and therefore you and your children's interests hinge on your ability to pierce the haze and make rational decisions.

Resist the impulse to settle scores with your wife on issues of custody. This means that you must compartmentalize your grievances and separate those meaningfully related to your children's welfare from those that are offenses to you personally, however grave.

Hopefully, you are not walking this path alone. In most cases, your attorney will be your key advisor, but many of the pivotal considerations are not within his province. Family members, friends, teachers and counselors can all lend support when times are tough.

Therefore, it is usually helpful to have the advice of others whose knowledge and judgment you respect. This may include a mental health professional, such as a counselor. However, if you choose this route, first talk to your attorney. Certain friends and family members may be helpful, but select from these pools carefully. Such "advisors" are notorious for pouring gasoline on the fire. Knowing who to tune in also means knowing who to tune out.

Divorce is a difficult time for the entire family. Staying focused on the ultimate goal—maximizing your time with your chldren—will make the process bearable.

Appendix 1: Petition for Dissolution

The petition is typically a short, simple, and legalistic document stating the basic facts and a request for the relief sought. This is described in Chapter 6.

IN THE CIRCUIT COURT OF
FAMILY COURT DIVISION
STATE OF

In Re the Marriage of	)	
	)	
JOHN DOE,	)	
SSN: 123-45-6789	)	
Petitioner,	)	
	)	Cause No.
vs.	)	
	)	Div.
JANE DOE,	)	
SSN: 987-65-4321	)	
SERVE: 123 Apple Street	)	
Anywhere, US 12345	)	
	)	
Respondent.	)	

PETITION FOR DISSOLUTION OF MARRIAGE

COMES NOW *JOHN DOE*, Petitioner, by and through his attorneys, and for his cause of action states:

1. Petitioner is and has been a resident of the State of for more than ninety (90) days immediately preceding the filing of this petition, now residing at 123 Orange Street, Anywhere.

2. Respondent is and has been a resident of the State of Missouri for more than ninety (90) days immediately preceding the filing of this petition, now residing at 123 Apple Street, Anywhere.

3. Petitioner's social security number is XXX-XX-XXXX and Respondent's social security number is XXX-XX-XXXX.

4. Petitioner is presently employed by (STATE EMPLOYER AND ADDRESS).

5. Respondent is presently employed by (STATE EMPLOYER AND

ADDRESS).

6. Petitioner and Respondent were married on January 1, 1999, and said marriage was registered at, the county of XXXXX, state of XXXXX.

7. Petitioner and Respondent separated on or about March 1, 1999.

8. Petitioner states that there is no reasonable likelihood that the marriage of Petitioner and Respondent can be preserved, and their marriage is therefore irretrievably broken.

9. There was one (1) minor child born of the marriage of Petitioner and Respondent; namely Jane Doe, Jr., born February 1, 1999, Social Security Number XXX-XX-XXXX; Respondent is not now pregnant.

10. The said minor child has lived in the custody of both Petitioner and Respondent. For the six months prior to said date, said minor child lived in the custody of Respondent.

(a) Petitioner has not participated in any capacity in any other litigation concerning the custody of said minor child.

(b) Petitioner has no information of any custody proceeding concerning the minor child herein pending in a court of this or any other state.

© Petitioner knows of no person not a party to these proceedings who has physical custody of said minor children, or claims to have custody or visitation rights with respect to said minor children.

11. Petitioner and Respondent have not participated in a previous action for dissolution. Petitioner is not aware of any other actions concerning the custody of said children in this state or any other.

12. It is in the best interests of said minor child that Petitioner be granted primary physical and sole legal custody of said minor child, subject to the custody schedule set forth in the Parenting Plan marked as Exhibit "A", attached hereto and incorporated herein.

13. Petitioner is possessed of certain items of property which are his separate property.

14. Petitioner and Respondent have accumulated property during the course of the marriage, as well as certain obligations and Petitioner requests that the marital property and debts be divided in a fair and equitable manner.

15. No arrangements as to the support of either party or the minor child have been made.

16. Petitioner does not have sufficient means with which to provide suit monies to prosecution of this action or money to secure costs that may accrue herein.

17. Respondent is able-bodied and is earning a substantial income, sufficient to enable her to provide Petitioner such sums of money as will enable him to employ counsel to represent him in the prosecution of this action and to provide suit monies and to secure the Court costs herein.

18. Neither Petitioner nor Respondent are a member of the Armed Forces of the United States.

WHEREFORE, Petitioner prays that the Court hear and determine this cause, and, upon such hearing, the Court make a finding that the marriage of the parties is irretrievably broken and the Court order; that the Court award to Petitioner the sole legal and primary physical care, custody and control of the minor child, subject to the visitation schedule set forth in the Parenting Plan marked as Exhibit "A"; that the marital property and marital debts be divided in a fair and equitable manner; that Petitioner's separate property be set aside to Petitioner; that Petitioner be awarded his attorneys' fees and costs incurred in this proceeding; and that for such other and further orders, judgments and decrees as may deem just and proper in the premises.

BY:__________________________
John Doe, Pro Se
123 Orange Street
Anywhere 12345
Telephone (XXX) XXX-XXXX
Facsimile (XXX) XXX-XXXX

Appendix 2: Answer to Petition for Dissolution

The answer admits or denies each assertion in the petition and will ask the court to deny the petitioner's request. This is described in Chapter 6.

IN THE CIRCUIT COURT OF
FAMILY COURT DIVISION
STATE OF

In Re the Marriage of	)	
	)	
JANE DOE,	)	
SSN: 123-45-6789	)	
Petitioner,	)	
	)	Cause No.
vs.	)	
	)	Div.
JOHN DOE,	)	
SSN: 987-65-4321	)	
	)	
Respondent.	)	

RESPONDENT'S ANSWER TO PETITIONER'S PETITION FOR DISSOLUTION OF MARRIAGE AND RESPONDENT'S CROSS-PETITION FOR DISSOLUTION OF MARRIAGE

ANSWER

COMES NOW Respondent, John Doe, and for his answer to Petitioner's Petition for Dissolution of Marriage states to the Court as follows:

1. Respondent admits/denies the allegations contained in paragraph 1.
2. Respondent admits/denies the allegations contained in paragraph 2.
3. Respondent admits/denies the allegations contained in paragraph 3.
4. Respondent admits/denies the allegations contained in paragraph 4.
5. Respondent admits/denies the allegations contained in paragraph 5
6. Respondent admits/denies the allegations contained in paragraph 6.
7. Respondent admits/denies the allegations contained in paragraph 7.
8. Respondent admits/denies the allegations contained in paragraph 8.
9. Respondent admits/denies the allegations contained in paragraph 9.

10. Respondent admits/denies the allegations contained in paragraph 10.

11. Respondent admits//denies the allegations contained in paragraph 11.

12. Respondent admits/denies the allegations contained in paragraph 12.

13. Respondent admits/denies the allegations contained in paragraph 13.

14. Respondent admits/denies the allegations contained in paragraph 14.

15. Respondent admits/denies the allegations contained in paragraph 15.

WHEREFORE, having fully answered, Respondent moves to dismiss Petitioner's Petition for Dissolution of Marriage and proceed on Respondent's Cross-Petition for Dissolution of Marriage; and for such other and further orders which to the Court seem just and proper in the premises.

CROSS-PETITION FOR DISSOLUTION OF MARRIAGE

COMES NOW Respondent, John Doe, and for his Cross-Petition for Dissolution of Marriage, states to the Court as follows:

1. Respondent has been a resident of the State of XXXXXXX for more than ninety (90) days next preceding the commencement of this action, and his address is 123 Orange Street, Anywhere. Petitioner has been a resident of the State of XXXXXX for more than ninety (90) days next preceding the commencement of this action, her current address is 123 Apple Street, Anywhere.

2. Petitioner is employed at STATE EMPLOYER AND ADDRESS and her Social Security Number is XXX-XX-XXXX. Respondent is presently employed by STATE EMPLOYER AND ADDRESS, and his Social Security Number is XXX-XX-XXXX.

3. Petitioner and Respondent were married on January 1, 1999, in the City of

XXXXXX and said marriage is registered in the County of XXXXXX, State of XXXXXX.

4. Petitioner and Respondent separated on or about March 1, 1999.

5. There was one child born of the marriage of Petitioner and Respondent, namely, Jane Doe, Jr., born February 1, 1999. Petitioner is not now pregnant.

6. There is a no reasonable likelihood that the marriage of Petitioner and Respondent can be preserved and, therefore, the marriage is irretrievably broken.

7. Respondent is possessed of certain items of property which are his separate property.

8. The parties are possessed of real property.

9. Petitioner is an able-bodied woman who is gainfully employed at a substantial wage and who is capable of providing for the support of herself and said minor child, and therefore, Petitioner requires no maintenance or child support from Respondent.

10. That Petitioner and Respondent have accumulated property during the course of the marriage, as well as certain obligations and Respondent requests that the marital property and debts be divided in a fair and equitable manner.

11. Neither Petitioner nor Respondent are members of the Armed Forces of the United States or any of its allies.

12. That the Respondent is without sufficient funds with which to pay his attorney's fees and costs of this action.

13. That Respondent shall be granted primary physical and sole custody of the minor child, Jane Doe, Jr.

WHEREFORE, Respondent prays that the Court dismiss Petitioner's Petition for Dissolution of Marriage and grant Respondent's Cross-Petition for Dissolution of Marriage; that the Court set apart to Respondent his separate property and divide equitably between the parties their marital property and debts; that Petitioner be ordered to pay Respondent's attorney fees and the costs of this action; that the parties share joint physical and joint legal custody of the said minor child; and that the Court make such other and further orders as are just and proper.

BY:______________________________
John Doe, Pro Se
123 Orange Street
Anywhere 12345
Telephone (XXX) XXX-XXXX
Facsimile (XXX) XXX-XXXX

STATE OF XXXXXX)
) SS
COUNTY OF XXXXX)

Comes now John Doe, Respondent, and upon his oath deposes and states:

1. He is over 18 years of age and is the Respondent herein.
2. He has read the foregoing Answer to Petitioner's Petition for Dissolution and Respondent's Cross-Petition for Dissolution of Marriage and states that it is true to the best of his knowledge and belief.

____
JOHN DOE

Subscribed and sworn to before me, a notary public, this ____ day of _________, 1999.

____
Notary Public

My Commission Expires:

Appendix 3: Exhibits

The evidence relating to maintenance and property division normally includes various financial documents. These are discussed in Chapter 6.

IN THE CIRCUIT COURT OF

IN RE THE MARRIAGE OF:

____
PETITIONER

VS

____
RESPONDENT

____
DATE

____
CASE NUMBER

____
TEAM/DIVISION

STATEMENT OF INCOME AND EXPENSES OF

____
NAME

____
SOCIAL SECURITY NUMBER

1. **INCOME**

A. Name and address of employer ______________________________

____

Gross Wages or Salary and commission each Pay Period .... $ ________

PAID: ________ Weekly ________ biweekly ________ semi-monthly ________ monthly

Number of dependents claimed ________

Payroll Deductions:

FICA (social Security Tax) .... $ ________

Federal Withholding Tax .... ________

State Withholding Tax .... ________

City Earnings Tax .... ________

Union Dues .... ________

Others:

______________________________ .... ________

______________________________ .... ________

Total Deductions each Pay Period .... $ ________

Net take home pay each pay period .... $ ________

B. Additional Income from Rentals, Dividends and Business Enterprises, Social Security, A.F.D.C. V.A. Benefits, Pensions, Annuities, Bonuses, "Commissions and all other sources (give monthly average and list sources of income).

______________________ .... ____________

______________________ .... ____________

______________________ .... ____________

______________________ .... ____________

Average Monthly Total .... $ ____________

C. Total Average Net Monthly Income .... $ ____________

D. Your share of the gross income shown on last year's Federal Income Tax Return .... $ ____________

2. Expenses required to maintain previous standard of living stated on a MONTHLY average

A. Rent or mortgage payments .... $ ____________

B. Utilities

1. Gas .... $ ____________

2. Water .... ____________

3. Electricity .... ____________

4. Telephone .... ____________

5. Trash Service .... ____________ $ ____________

C. Automobiles

1. Gas and Oil .... $ ____________

2. Maintenance (routine) .... ____________

3. Taxes and License .... ____________

4. Payment on the Auto Loan .... ____________ $ ____________

D. Insurance

1. Life .... $ ____________

2. Health & Accident .... ____________

3. Disability .... ____________

4. Homeowners (if not included in mortgage payment) $ ____________

5. Automobile .... ____________ $ ____________

E. Total payment installments Contracts .... $ ______

F. Child Support Paid to Others for children not in your Custody (excluding children of this marriage) .... $ ______

G. Maintenance or Alimony (excluding Petitioner or Respondent herein) .... $ ______

H. Church and Charitable Contributions .... $ ______

I. Other Living Expenses (total of items 1 - 7 listed below) .... $ ______

	Yours	Children in your custody
1. Food	$ ______	$ ______
2. Clothing	______	______
3. Medical Care, Dental Care and Drugs	______	______
4. Recreation	______	______
5. Laundry and Cleaning	______	______
6. Barber Shop or Beauty Shop	______	______
7. School and Books	______	______
....	$ ______	$ ______

J. Day Care Center or Babysitter .... $ ______

K. All other Expenses Not Presently Identified - (give as a monthly average)

______ .... $ ______

______ .... ______

______ .... ______

______ .... ______

L. Total Average Monthly Expenses .... $ ______

STATE OF
COUNTY OF , SS.

Comes now ____,
being of lawful age and after being duly sworn, states that affiant has read the foregoing Statement of Income and Expenses, and that the facts therein are true and correct according to the affiant's best knowledge and belief.

____
Affiant

Subscribed and sworn to before me, the undersigned Notary Public on this ______________ day of

______________________, 19 ______.

My Commission Expires:

______________________ ______________________________
Notary Public

I hereby certify that I mailed a copy of this Statement of Income and Expense to ______________________

______________________________, an attorney for the (Petitioner) (Respondent) by

depositing a copy thereof in the United States Mail, postage pre-paid, this ______________ day of

______________________, 19 ______

____

IN THE CIRCUIT COURT OF

IN RE THE MARRIAGE OF:

PETITIONER

VS

RESPONDENT

DATE

CASE NUMBER

TEAM/DIVISION

STATEMENT OF PROPERTY

NAME

SOCIAL SECURITY NUMBER

I. **PROPERTY** (include all marital property and separate property of both parties and designate owner of separate property)	Present Value	Amount Owed	Marital or Separate Property*
A. **Real Estate** - list any and all interests held in real estate (include legal description and name of mortgagor).			
B. **Motor Vehicles** (including all automobiles, boats, trailers, aircraft recreational vehicles and campers, and give year, make, model, and serial number and name of mortgagor).			
C. **Bank Accounts** - List all checking and savings accounts held either in your name alone or in your name and that of another person. Give the name of the institution, the names on the account and the account number. Be sure to include here all time deposit, etc.			

* Indicate whether marital or separate property and if separate, also indicate whether received by gift, inheritance, owned before marriage or exchanged for such.

	Present Value	Amount Owed	Marital or Separate Property*
K. **Any Interest in a Contract made but not yet performed** - List the parties to the contract, their address and the expected date of performance, if any.			
L. **Any Interest in Pending Litigation or Suits yet to be filed.**			
M. **Any Interest in Farm Equipment, Animals, or Crops** - give nature of the property and its location.			
N. **Any debt owed to you by others** - List the name and address of the debtor, any security, date of loan and due date, if any, etc.			
O. **Future Interests** - List the interest you hold, the property involved and the present owner.			
P. **Partnership Interests** - (list the name of partners and percentage interest). Attach a copy of the partnership agreement or set forth its terms with assets and liabilities.			
Q. **List any other Asset not already listed herein.**			

* Indicate whether marital or separate property and if separate, also indicate whether received by gift, inheritance, owned before marriage or exchanged for such.

II. DEBTS	Current Balance	Monthly Payments
A. List all loans from any bank or lending institution to you. Show who signed the loan, the date of the loan, and give the name and address of the lender and the outstanding balance. ____________________ ____________________ ____________________ ____________________ ____________________	$	$
B. List all credit card balances and store charges - Show the name on the credit card. ____________________ ____________________ ____________________ ____________________ ____________________	$	$
C. Other indebtedness - Show to whom and purpose of loan. ____________________ ____________________ ____________________ ____________________ ____________________	$	$

STATE OF
COUNTY OF ST. LOUIS

Comes now, ____________________, being of lawful age and after being duly sworn, states that affiant has read the foregoing Statement of Property and the facts therein are true and correct according to the affiant's best knowledge and belief and that all property has been included.

____
Affiant

Subscribed and sworn to before me the undersigned Notary Public, on this ________ day of ________ ________________, 19 ______.

My Commission expires: ____________________

____
NOTARY PUBLIC

I hereby certify that I mailed a copy of this Statement of Property to ____________________, attorney for (Petitioner) (Respondent) by depositing a copy thereof in the United States Mail, postage prepaid, this ____________ day of ____________________, 19 ______.

Appendix 4:
Parenting Plan

Most jurisdictions have a standard custodial or parenting plan addressing both legal and physical custody. This appendix shows the form adopted by St. Louis County, Missouri. Parenting plans are discussed in Chapter 7.

IN THE FAMILY COURT OF

______________________,	)	__________	For File Stamp Only
Petitioner,	)	Date	
VS	)	__________	
	)	Case No.	
______________________,	)	__________	
Respondent.	)	Division	

PARENTING PLAN - BASIC

Physical Custody (and Visitation)

1. Custody, visitation and residential time for each child with each parent shall be at such times as the parties agree. In the event that the parties cannot agree **(Father)(Mother)*** [hereinafter "parent B"] shall have custody, visitation or residential time as set forth below in sub-paragraphs "A", "B", "C" and "D", the other parent [hereinafter "parent A"] having all other time as his or her custody, visitation or residential time. [Except as provided otherwise in Appendix A attached ☐ if box checked.] [If there are restrictions or limitations on access to a party, check the box ☐ and in Appendix A state the reasons for the restriction.]

A. Weekend: Every other weekend beginning at 6:00 pm on Friday through and ending at 6:00 pm on Sunday; beginning the weekend following the date of the judgment. If either parent's holiday weekend, as set forth below in sub-paragraph "D", conflicts herewith then the parent losing their regular weekend shall receive the other parent's next regular weekend to thereafter be followed by the original schedule so that each would have 2 consecutive weekends.

B. Weekday: One night each week from 5:00 pm on Wednesday until 8:00 am on Thursday.

C. Summer: Six weeks each summer (to be divided into three 14 consecutive day periods) to coincide with the child(ren)'s school summer vacation. Until at least one child is in school the summer vacation period shall be during the months June, July and August. Parent B may select the first two weeks of this summer vacation by notifying parent A of same (each notification herein to be in writing) by February 1st each year, two weeks may then be excluded by parent A by March 1st, the next two weeks may be selected by parent B by April 1st, two more weeks may then be excluded by parent A by May 1st, the final two weeks may be selected by parent B by June 1st. Parent A's excluded four weeks shall prevail over parent B's weekend and weekday periods set forth in sub-paragraph A and B above.

D. Holidays:

1. Holidays and special days herein shall prevail over weekend, weekday and summer vacation set forth in sub-paragraphs "A", "B" and "C" above. Birthday periods shall not prevail when in conflict with other Holiday and Special Days.

2. Mother shall have custody or visitation with the child(ren) on her birthday and on Mother's Day each year from 9:00 am to 9:00 pm; plus "Holiday Group A" in even-numbered years and "Holiday Group B" in odd-numbered years.

3. Father shall have custody or visitation with the child(ren) on his birthday and on Father's Day each year from 9:00 am to 9:00 pm; plus "Holiday Group A" in odd-numbered years and "Holiday Group B" in even-numbered years.

** Strike word not applicable.*

Holiday Group A

1. PRESIDENT'S DAY / WASHINGTON'S BIRTHDAY (OBSERVED) weekend from 5:00 pm the Friday prior through 8:00 am the following Tuesday.

2. A period of 7 days during the child(ren)'s school Spring break, the exact days to be selected and written notice given to the other party not later than 30 days prior to the start thereof. Until at least one child is in school this 7 day period shall begin at 8:00 am the Monday before Easter Sunday and shall end at 6:00 pm on Easter Sunday.

3. INDEPENDENCE DAY (July 4th) holiday from 5:00 pm the next non-weekend day before to 9:00 am the weekday next following.

4. COLUMBUS DAY weekend from 5:00 pm the Friday prior through 8:00 am the following Tuesday.

5. CHRISTMAS vacation from December 25th beginning at 10:00 am through 9:00 am on December 31st.

6. Each child's birthday from 9:00 am until 9:00 am the following day.

Holiday Group B

1. MARTIN LUTHER KING weekend from 5:00 pm the Friday prior through 8:00 am the following Tuesday.

2. MEMORIAL DAY weekend from 5:00 pm the Friday prior through 8:00 am the following Tuesday.

3. LABOR DAY weekend from 5:00 pm the Friday prior through 8:00 am the following Tuesday.

4. THANKSGIVING weekend from 5:00 pm the Wednesday prior through 8:00 am the following Monday.

5. CHRISTMAS vacation from 5:00 pm the day the child(ren)'s school Christmas vacation begins through 10:00 am on December 25th and December 31st beginning at 9:00 am through 8:00 am the day the child(ren)'s school Christmas vacation ends. Until at least one child is in school the Christmas period shall begin December 23rd and end January 3rd.

6. The day prior to each child's birthday beginning at 9:00 am through 9:00 am the day of the birthday.

E. Notice If Unavailable to Exercise Custody or Visitation: In the event either parent will not be able to exercise the scheduled custody or visitation period he or she shall so advise the other parent at the earliest possible opportunity, but not later than 24 hours prior to the scheduled start of the custody or visitation period unless the parent unable to exercise his or her period has previously, earlier than 24 hours, advised the other parent that he or she has a potential conflict that may at the last minute make it impossible to exercise the scheduled custody or visitation period. [Except as provided otherwise in Appendix A attached ☐ if box checked].

F. Transportation: Unless the parties agree otherwise, the child(ren) shall, at the beginning of each custody or visitation period, be picked up from and, at the end of each custody or visitation period, be returned to the residence parent A by parent B at parent B's expense [except as provided otherwise in Appendix A attached ☐ if box checked.

G. Telephone Contact: Each parent shall inform the other of his or her residence address and telephone number, the address and telephone number of his or her place of employment, and in the event of extended out-of-town travel, the address and telephone number of his or her destination. The duty to update this information is a continuing obligation and shall be done within a reasonable time after any change. Each party shall have reasonable telephone access with the child(ren) during normal waking hours during any period in which the child(ren) is(are) with the other parent. [Except as provided otherwise in Appendix A attached ☐ if box checked.]

H. Changes To Schedule: Recognizing the needs of the child(ren) for a continuing relationship with each parent, each parent shall exercise their best efforts to foster the respect, love and affections of the child(ren) toward the other parent and shall avoid any action which would demean the other parent before the child(ren). To the extent possible the parties shall accommodate the social and academic commitments of the child(ren) and shall cooperate to insure that the child(ren) shall have regular and frequent contact with each parent. In that regard each party shall reasonably consider any requests made by the other party to change the scheduled custody or visitation periods previously agreed when a timely request is made for the change by a party or the child(ren). There shall be no restrictions or limitations on the child(ren)'s reasonable access to either parent. [Except as provided otherwise in Appendix A attached ☐ if box checked.]

Legal Custody

2. If a parent is awarded sole legal custody he or she shall confer with and seek input from the parent not awarded legal custody, and if the parents are awarded joint legal custody, or before the entry of a Family Court Judgment they shall agree, before making any final decisions on issues affecting the growth and development of the child(ren); including, but not limited to, choice of religious upbringing, choice of child care provider, choice of school, course of study, special tutoring, extracurricular activities, including but not limited to, music, art, dance and other cultural lessons or activities and gymnastics or other athletic activities, choice of camp or other comparable summer activity, non-emergency medical and dental treatment, psychological, psychiatric or like treatment or counseling, the choice of particular health care providers, the extent of any travel away from home, part or full-time employment, purchase or operation of a motor vehicle, contraception and sex education, and decisions relating to actual or potential litigation on behalf of the child(ren). However, each parent may make decisions regarding the day-to-day care and control of the child(ren) and in emergencies affecting the health and safety of the child(ren) while the child(ren) is(are) residing with him or her. The parents shall endeavor, whenever reasonable, to be consistent in such day-to-day decisions. [Except as provided otherwise in Appendix B attached ☐ if box checked.] [If there is to be sole legal custody, check the box ☐ and in Appendix B state the reasons where there should be no shared decision-making.]

A. Communication: Each parent shall insure that the other parent is provided with copies of all communications or information received from a child's school, and if a second copy of the communication is not provided by the school shall make a copy for the other parent. Each parent shall notify the other of any activity such as school conferences, programs, sporting and other special events etc., where parents are invited to attend and each shall encourage and welcome the presence of the other. [Except as provided otherwise in Appendix B attached ☐ if box checked.]

B. Medical Care Information: Each parent shall advise the other of any medical emergency or serious illness or injury suffered by the child(ren) when in his or her custody or during visitation as soon as possible after learning of the same and shall give the other parent the details of said emergency, injury or illness and the name and telephone number of the attending physician(s), if any. Each parent will inform the other before any routine medical care, treatment or examination by a health care provider including said provider's name, address and telephone number. Each party shall direct all doctors involved in any care and treatment of the child(ren) to give the other parent all information regarding any medical treatment or examination, if requested by a parent. [Except as provided otherwise in Appendix B attached ☐ if box checked.]

C. Child Care Provider: If both parents will need to use a child care provider during periods of custody or visitation they shall use the same child care provider, unless the distances between their residences or places of employment make the use of the same child care provider unreasonable. If one party has been awarded sole physical custody, the child care provider shall be selected by the parent with sole physical custody after input from the other parent. [Except as provided otherwise in Appendix B attached ☐ if box checked.]

D. Access To Records: Each parent shall be entitled to immediate access from the other or from a third party to records and information pertaining to the child(ren) including, but not limited to, medical, dental, health, child care, school or educational records; and each shall take whatever steps necessary to insure that the other parent has such access [except as provided otherwise in Appendix B attached ☐ if box checked].

E. Activities To Not Conflict With Custody or Visitation: If either parent is awarded sole legal custody he or she shall enroll the child(ren) in activities, particularly outside of school, which, to the extent possible, are scheduled at times and places which avoid interruption and disruption of the custody or visitation time of the parent not awarded legal custody of the child(ren) unless consented to by that parent. In that regard, each child shall not be enrolled in more than one activity at a time that has routinely scheduled practices, games or other events during the custody or visitation time of the parent without legal custody without that parent's consent if he or she routinely exercises most of the awarded custody or visitation time. [Except as provided otherwise in Appendix B attached ☐ if box checked.]

F. Mediation Of Disputes: In the event the parties are awarded joint legal custody and they are unable to agree upon a final decision on issues affecting the growth and development or health and safety of the child(ren), as provided for herein, they shall submit the dispute to a mutually agreed mediator. In the event they are not able to agree on a mediator they shall each select a mediator from the list of approved mediators maintained by the St. Louis County Family Court. The two selected mediators shall then select from the same list a mediator to help the parties resolve the dispute. In the event that the parties cannot resolve the dispute by mediation they may file a motion and submit the issue to the Court. [Except as provided otherwise in Appendix B attached ☐ if box checked.]

Support

3. Child support shall be paid by the parent obligated to pay support (hereinafter "paying parent") to the parent entitled to receive support (hereinafter "receiving parent") as set forth in the Family Court Judgment [or if there is no Family Court Judgment the presumed child support amount per the attached Form 14 ☐ if box checked]. If the child support is expressed per month it shall be paid 50% on the first and 50% on the 16th day of each month; and if the child support is expressed per week it shall be paid on the Friday of each week. [Except as provided otherwise in Appendix C attached ☐ if box checked.]

A. Health Care Costs: The paying parent, unless the parties agree or the Family Court Judgment provides otherwise, shall maintain at his or her cost a health benefit plan covering the child(ren). All health expenses incurred on behalf of the child(ren) by either parent who has joint legal custody, or with consent of the parent with sole legal, and not paid by the health benefit plan shall be paid fifty percent (50%) by each parent if incurred pursuant to the health benefit plan. If a parent incurs an expense to a health care provider that is not covered by the health benefit plan that would have been covered, or covered at a more favorable rate, if a provider included in the plan had been used, then that parent shall pay seventy-five percent (75%) and the other parent twenty-five percent (25%) of the uncovered expenses. Provided however, the receiving parent shall pay one-hundred percent (100%) of the first $100 of health care expenses per year for each child incurred by a parent with joint or sole legal custody. [Except as provided otherwise in Appendix C attached ☐ if box checked.]

B. Education and Extraordinary Expenses: If a parent has sole legal custody he or she shall pay the educational and extraordinary expenses of the child(ren) unless the parties agree or the Family Court Judgment provides otherwise. If the parents have joint legal custody they shall each pay fifty percent (50%) of the educational and extraordinary expenses that are incurred by agreement unless the parties agree or the Family Court Judgment provides otherwise. [Except as provided otherwise in Appendix C attached ☐ if box checked.]

C. Child Care Expenses: Unless the parties agree or the Family Court Judgment provides otherwise, child care expenses shall be paid by the receiving parent. If the paying parent elects to obtain child care from a child care provider other than the provider used by the receiving parent during his or her periods of custody or visitation, the paying parent shall pay the expenses for the child care costs he or she so incurs. [Except as provided otherwise in Appendix C attached ☐ if box checked.]

D. Child(ren) Not Involved In Court or Financial Communications: All court related and financial communications between the parents shall occur at a time when the child(ren) is(are) not present and, therefore, shall not occur at times of exchanges of the child(ren) or during telephone visits with the child(ren). Furthermore the child(ren) shall not be used to deliver any such court related or financial communication between the parents. [Except as provided otherwise in Appendix C attached ☐ if box checked.]

Enclosures: (If attached, check box below and above as appropriate. Paragraphs in an Appendix shall be numbered the same as the corresponding paragraph in the Parenting Plan to which they relate.)

- ☐ Appendix A - Physical Custody (and Visitation)
- ☐ Appendix B - Legal Custody
- ☐ Appendix C - Support
- ☐ Form 14

Petitioner	Respondent	
Attorney for Petitioner	Attorney for Respondent	Guardian ad litem

Appendix 5: Order of Protection

Orders of Protection and when they are used is discussed in Chapter 10.

IN THE FAMILY COURT OF ST. LOUIS COUNTY, MISSOURI

DIVISION	COURT ORI NUMBER **MO.0RI095015J**
	CASE NUMBER

PETITIONER VS. D.O.B., AGE OR SOC. SEC #:	PETITIONER'S HOME ADDRESS: (UNLESS DISCLOSURE WAIVED)

(DATE FILE STAMP)

RESPONDENT D.O.B., AGE OR SOC. SEC # SEX [ ] F [ ] M RACE: EYE COLOR: HAIR COLOR: HEIGHT: WEIGHT:	RESPONDENT'S HOME AND WORK ADDRESS: RESPONDENT'S RELATIONSHIP TO PETITIONER: [ ] SPOUSE [ ] EX-SPOUSE [ ] RELATED BY BLOOD/MARRIAGE [ ] CHILD IN COMMON [ ] RESIDED TOGETHER [ ] OTHER________

APPEARANCES: [ ] PETITIONER [ ] PETITIONER'S ATTORNEY [ ] RESPONDENT [ ] RESPONDENT'S ATTORNEY [ ] OTHER______

ADULT ABUSE
JUDGMENT/FULL ORDER OF PROTECTION

Also used for Consent Order and Extensions of Full Order of Protection

(Check Applicable Statement)

[ ] The petitioner has filed a petition requesting issuance of an order of protection and a notice was served together with a copy of the petition to the respondent at least three days prior to the hearing. The matter heard and submitted to Court, and upon due consideration of the matter, the Court finds pursuant to Section 455.040 RSMo that the petitioner has proved the allegations of abuse or stalking.

[ ] The petitioner and respondent submit this Consent Judgment and request that the Court order the following:

______________________**ORDER (Only Those Provisions Checked Apply)**______________________

[ ] This order replaces and supersedes the ex parte order of protection entered in this cause on (date) ____________, and serves as notice of termination of that order.

[ ] Respondent shall not stalk, abuse, threaten to abuse, molest or disturb the peace of petitioner wherever the petitioner may be.

[ ] Respondent shall not enter or stay upon premises of the dwelling of petitioner, located at________________

____ **[08]**

[ ] Respondent shall not transfer, encumber or otherwise dispose of the following property mutually owned or leased with petitioner:____ **[08]**

[ ] Petitioner to be given temporary possession of the following personal property:________________

____

[ ] Respondent shall participate in the court approved counseling program for
[ ] batterers [ ] substance abuse treatment at________________beginning________.

[ ] Custody of child(ren) is awarded as follows: **[RESPONDENT- 06, PETITIONER-08]:**

Child's Name and Date of Birth	Person to Receive Custody
________________	________________
________________	________________
________________	________________

CCFC36 Rev 01/98 Page 1 of 2

White - File Green - Police Yellow - Respondent Pink - Sheriff's/Police Goldenrod - Petitioner

[ ] The following visitation schedule is established: (☐ Per Exhibit ________________ Attached

____

____

[ ] Respondent to pay child support to petitioner as follows: $ ____________________ per child per ________________

with first payment due (date) ____

[ ] Respondent to pay maintenance to petitioner as follows: $ ______________________________ per month/week

with first payment due (date) ____

[ ] (Petitioner)(Respondent) shall execute an income assignment in favor of (Petitioner)(Respondent) for
[ ] child support [ ] maintenance

[ ] Respondent to pay petitioner's rent or mortgage in the amount of $ ________________ per ________________ to

________________________________ with first payment due (date) ________________________

[ ] Respondent shall pay for housing or other services provided to the petitioner by shelter for victims of domestic violence in the

amount of $ __________________ per________________ to ________________________________

with first payment due (date) ____

[ ] (Petitioner)(Respondent) shall pay to the (Petitioner)(Respondent) the amount of $ __________________________ for the cost of maintaining or defending this action

[ ] (Petitioner)(Respondent) shall pay to the (Petitioner)(Respondent) attorney's fees in the amount of $ ________________.

[ ] The court (a) finds you are a credible threat to the physical safety of the petitioner who is/was an intimate partner. OR
(b) by this order, explicitly prohibits the use, attempted use, or threatened use of physical force against such intimate partner or child that would reasonably be expected to cause bodily injury.
NOTE: THIS MAY PROHIBIT THE POSSESSION OF A FIREARM UNDER FEDERAL STATUTE. (SEE NOTICE ON REVERSE).

[ ] Other Orders: ____

____

____

____

____

____

____

____

____

[ ] Court costs are to be paid by: [Petitioner] [Respond] [Equally] [Waived]

THIS ORDER SHALL BE EFFECTIVE UNTIL (DATE) ________________________, UNLESS SOONER TERMINATED OR EXTENDED.

VIOLATION OF THIS ORDER MAY BE PUNISHED BY CONFINEMENT IN JAIL FOR AS LONG AS FIVE YEARS AND BY A FINE OF AS MUCH AS FIVE THOUSAND DOLLARS.

________________________________ SO ORDERED: ________________________________
DATE JUDGE

CONSENT ORDER ONLY

This consent is not to be taken as an admission by respondent that the allegations contained in the petition are true; however, respondent consents to the above orders being issued.

________________________________ ________________________________
PETITIONER'S SIGNATURE RESPONDENT'S SIGNATURE

CCFC36 Rev. 01/98 Page 2 of 2

White - File Green - Police Yellow - Respondent Pink - Sheriff's/Police Goldenrod - Petitioner

INSTRUCTIONS TO CLERK

1. A copy of the order of protection shall be issued to the petitioner, the respondent, and the law enforcement agency (police or sheriff) in the city or county where the petitioner resides.
2. A copy of the order of protection shall be issued the same day the order is granted to the law enforcement agency responsible for maintaining the Missouri Uniform Law Enforcement System (MULES).
3. A copy of the order of protection shall be served upon or mailed by certified mail to the respondent(s) at their last known address.

NOTICE TO THE PERSON OBLIGATED TO PAY SUPPORT OR MAINTENANCE
(Pursuant to Section 452.350)

Effective January 1, 1994, for every order for child support or maintenance entered or modified by the court under the authority of Chapter 452 or otherwise, income withholding under Section 452.350 RSMo shall be initiated on the effective date of the order unless the court finds there is good reason not to require immediate income withholding or a written agreement between the parties provides for an alternative arrangement.

NOTICE REGARDING FIREARMS RESTRICTIONS PER FEDERAL LAW

Pursuant to 18 USC 922

(g) It shall be unlawful for any person-

(8) who is subject to a court order that-

(A) was issued after a hearing of which such person received actual notice, and at which such person had an opportunity to participate;

(B) restrains such person from harassing, stalking, or threatening an intimate partner of such person or child of such intimate partner or person, or engaging in other conduct that would place an intimate partner in reasonable fear of bodily injury to the partner or child; and

(C)(i) includes a finding that such person represents a credible threat to the physical safety of such intimate partner or child; or

(ii) by its terms explicitly prohibits the use, attempted use, or threatened use of physical force against such intimate partner or child that would reasonably be expected to cause bodily injury,

to ship or transport in interstate or foreign commerce, or possess in or affecting commerce, any firearm or ammunition; or to receive any firearm or ammunition which has been shipped or transported in interstate or foreign commerce.

SHERIFF'S OR SERVER'S RETURN (Not Required for Consent Order)

I certify that I served a copy of this order by delivering a copy to the respondent

Served at (address) ______________________________

on (date) ______________________________ at (time) ____________ M.

SHERIFF'S FEES (If applicable)

Service Fee $____________ Mileage $__________ (__________ miles @ $ __________ per mile)

Non Est $____________ Total $__________

____
SHERIFF

CCFC36 Rev. 01/98

About Our Firm

Cordell & Cordell was founded in 1990. Originally a general practice firm focusing its attention on domestic relations matters, Cordell & Cordell has evolved into a firm practicing exclusively domestic relations law, with an overwhelming emphasis on fathers' rights. Men represent approximately 98% of our clientele. As of the printing of this book, our offices had spread to twelve cities in the states of Missouri, Illinois, Kansas, Georgia, Indiana, Texas and Colorado with our corporate headquarters based out of St. Louis. We presently employ 34 lawyers and to date have served thousands of men.

Cordell & Cordell is one of the largest firms of its kind in the US. We market and advertise ourselves as a firm devoted to men's interests. The website we sponsor, www.dadsdivorce.com, is one of the most comprehensive sites on the Web for information relating to dads and custody.

Cordell & Cordell aggressively champions the causes of divorcing fathers. Too often lawyers, and even judges, have resigned themselves to stereotypes and a perpetuation of the status quo. The result is that the judicial system (i.e., lawyers, judges, social workers, and the administration) is prone to assume without proof that moms should be the primary custodial parents, that men accused of abuse are guilty of abuse, that men alleging abuse are lying or overreacting,

No law firm can completely rectify these deep-seeded biases, but at Cordell & Cordell, we have cultivated a reputation for challenging fallacious assumptions, and for calling the court's attention to inequalities. In addition, at Cordell & Cordell we teach our clients steps they can take to maximize their chances of receiving the greatest amount of time and participation in their children's lives while minimizing any financial drain.

Index